Guaranteed Formula
for

Public Speaking Success

by
Everett Ofori, MBA

CCB Publishing
British Columbia, Canada

Guaranteed Formula for Public Speaking Success

Copyright ©2011 by Everett Ofori
ISBN-13   978-1-926918-92-1
First Edition

Library and Archives Canada Cataloguing in Publication
Ofori, Everett, 1963-
Guaranteed formula for public speaking success / written by Everett Ofori – 1st ed.
Includes bibliographical references and index.
ISBN 978-1-926918-92-1
Also available in electronic format.
1. Public speaking.   I. Title.
PN4129.15.O36 2011   808.5'1   C2011-906855-9

Illustrations: Ahn Soo Kyoung

Author contact: everettofori@gmail.com

Extreme care has been taken to ensure that all information presented in this book is accurate and up to date at the time of publishing.   The publisher cannot be held responsible for any errors or omissions.   Additionally, neither is any liability assumed for damages resulting from the use of the information contained herein.

All rights reserved. No part of this publication may be reproduced, stored in a retrieval system or transmitted in any form or by any means, electronic, mechanical, photocopying, recording or otherwise without the express written permission of the publisher, except in the case of brief quotations embodied in critical articles and reviews. Printed in the United States of America, the United Kingdom and Australia.

Publisher: CCB Publishing
                British Columbia, Canada
                www.ccbpublishing.com

*Dedicated to all who understand that **communication** is not just about **speaking** but also about **listening***

Other books by Everett Ofori

Succeeding From the Margins of Canadian Society:
A Strategic Resource for New Immigrants, Refugees
and International Students
Written by Francis Adu-Febiri and Everett Ofori
© 2009 – ISBN 978-1-926585-27-7

Read Assure:
Guaranteed Formula for Reading Success with Phonics
Written by Everett Ofori
© 2010 – ISBN 978-1-926585-83-3

Guaranteed Formula for Writing Success
Written by Everett Ofori
© 2011 – ISBN 978-1-926918-22-8

Acknowledgments

Thanks very much to Ms. Asta Lee and other members of the Hong Kong Toastmasters Club (Mr. Lap Wong, Mr. Edwin Lui, Ms. Tina Wong, *et al.*), who so impressed me with their dedication to communications excellence. Ms. Lee, evaluator par excellence, also shared with me some of her winning techniques, some of which have found their way into this book.

Members of Thames Valley Toastmasters Club, London, Ontario, Canada, under the leadership of Harold Usher; Thunderbird Toastmasters Club, Victoria, British Columbia, Canada; and Atsugi-Zama Toastmasters Club, Kanagawa, Japan, of which I count, Mr. Bruce Perkins, Mr. Tom Myslinski, Mr. Masashi Wada, Ms. Yuki Tateishi, Mr. Takamasa Sakuragi, Mr. Shintaro Inagaki, Ms. Yayoi Komura, Ms. Ai Tanaka, Mr. Masaru Horioka, Mr. Shigeru Maruyama, and Ms. Kanako Takayanagi, to name a few, have all been for me, models of commitment, persistence, and excellence.

My gratitude also goes to Mr. Kris Esplin of Phoenix Associates, Tokyo, Japan, who provided me with an opportunity to test out the techniques presented in this book in the real world: helping business executives to communicate effectively.

The support of Mr. Peter Owans, President and CEO of Phoenix Associates, Mr. Adrian Crawley, Mr. Yohei Akiyama, Ms. Megumi Matsuo, Ms. Hiroko Takagi, Mr. Shuji Yamada, Mr. Hiro Mikata, Ms. Candace Tarasawa, Ms. Saori Eto, and others, is noted with much gratitude.

Feedback from executive coaches and trainers who have used these materials, including Mr. John Anderson, Mr. Jon Southurst, Ms. Araminta Hammond, Dr. Vikas Sood, Ms. Diana Camargo, Mr. Robert Brinegar, Mr. Andrew Gleboff, Mr. Michael Mitchell, Mr. Ian Gordon, Ms. Gail Euen (who made numerous editorial suggestions), and others, is also very much appreciated.

Furthermore, I have benefited greatly from the scores of students who have used these materials and demonstrated through their efforts that there is value in expending the energy necessary to make one's dreams come true.

Many thanks to Ms. Diana Camargo, who used these materials several times, and proofread them for me. Similarly, Mr. Frank Pridgen brought his sharp editorial eyes to bear on the work. Still, as the author, I take full responsibility for any errors of omission or commission.

Introduction

Sooner or later, you will find yourself called upon to give a presentation or to "say a few words" at a party, a boardroom, or a rally. What you say on such an occasion may soon be forgotten but your inability to rise to the occasion may stay with you for a long time. Hopefully, your desire to become a better speaker is rooted less in the fear of such an eventuality and more in the desire to be a better communicator so that you can bring more light of understanding where none exists, contribute to a meeting of minds where people are working at cross-purposes, or bring a measure of goodness, grace, and greatness to your little corner of the world.

In practically every society, those who learn to communicate well are apt to become leaders — in their clubs or circles, communities, counties, or countries. Or they may become the ones that leaders turn to again and again for advice on how to communicate matters of local or national importance.

Whether in personal matters, business affairs, or political life, the ability to express oneself well in public is both a prized and powerful asset. While the mention of public speaking might strike fear into the hearts of men and women the world over, the good news is that it is a skill that can be improved with diligent effort.

The would-be speaker cannot hope to become proficient from reading books alone, yet the techniques and ideas picked up from books can help make the public speaking journey a far more enjoyable one.

Whether you are a public speaking novice or one with a few dozen speeches under your belt, I'm certain that you will find some new nuggets herein that will help you move closer to the ideal speaker you desire to be. Happy speaking!

Everett Ofori, MBA (Heriot-Watt University)
ACS (Advanced Communicator Silver - Toastmasters International)

Contents

Unit 1	First Things First: How to Use this Book	1
Unit 2	Impromptu Speech Organizing Framework 1: PPF	6
Unit 3	Impromptu Speech Organizing Framework 2: PREP	11
Unit 4	Impromptu Speech Organizing Framework 3: The Six-Finger Speaking Hand	15
Unit 5	Impromptu Speech Organizing Framework 4: IFONI	19
Unit 6	Impromptu Speech Organizing Framework 5: The Two-handed Mouth	22
Unit 7	Purpose of the Speech	27
Unit 8	Key Elements for Public Speaking	30
Unit 9	Common Public Speaking Problems	33
Unit 10	Positive Elements in Public Speaking	37
Unit 11	Know Your Audience	41
Unit 12	Good Organization: <u>Introduction</u>, Body, and Conclusion	43
Unit 13	Quick Introductions	46
Unit 14	Notes: To Use or Not to Use	50
Unit 15	Introduction to Speech Evaluation	54
Unit 16	The Sandwich Technique for Speech Evaluation	58
Unit 17	Sandwich Technique Template	62
Unit 18	The Speech Burger/Write Burger	64
Unit 19	How to Write a Speech…If You Must	66
Unit 20	Five Ways to Begin Your Speech	70
Unit 21	The Speech Burger – A Closer Look	73
Unit 22	Effective Conclusions	78
Unit 23	How to Introduce a Speaker	81
Unit 24	Introducing a Speaker: Preparation Sheet	84
Unit 25	Short-notice Speech Preparation	87
Unit 26	Speech Evaluation: The CR Technique	91
Unit 27	Evaluating the Evaluator	96
Unit 28	For the Mind's Eye: Painting Pictures	99
Unit 29	Speech Introductions: Using an Anecdote/Mini-story	103
Unit 30	Vocal Variety: Using the Greatest Musical Instrument	106

Unit 31	Connecting with the Audience	109
Unit 32	Visual Aids	113
Unit 33	Speech Evaluation: The IMGEPaC Technique	116
Unit 34	The Power of Persuasion	121
Unit 35	Can You Inspire? Moving to Higher Ground	125
Unit 36	Handling Questions and Answers	128
Unit 37	Making Numbers Make Sense	131
Unit 38	Speaking With an Eye on the Clock	134
Unit 39	Extemporaneous Speaking – The Pleasure and the Peril	136
Unit 40	Impromptu Speaking: Advanced Techniques 1	139
	● Problem + Solution	139
	● PRS: Problem, Reaction, Solution	140
	● PCS: Problem, Cause, Solution	141
Unit 41	Impromptu Speaking: Advanced Techniques 2	143
	● Bait and Switch: A Desperate Maneuver	143
	● What Would So-and-so Say about Such-and-such?	144
Unit 42	Impromptu Speaking: Advanced Techniques 3	148
	● PESTLE: Political, Economic, Social, Technological Legal, Environmental	148
	● SWOT: Strengths, Weaknesses, Opportunities, Threats	150
Unit 43	Speech Evaluation: The GLOVE Technique	153
Unit 44	When YOU are the Master of Ceremonies	155
Unit 45	The MC Role: Before the Event	157
Unit 46	The MC Role: During the Event	164
Unit 47	The MC Role: Bringing the Agenda to Life	168
Unit 48	The MC Role: After the Event	173
Unit 49	Public Speaking – Going Pro	174
Unit 50	Resources	177
Bibliography		179
Recommended Books		180
Useful Websites		181
Templates		182
100 Topics for Impromptu Speaking Practice		188
Index		190

Unit 1

First Things First: How to Use this Book

This book has a successful track record. It has been used to train businessmen and women who need to communicate frequently to groups of people as part of their job. Users of the techniques in this book have included those with practically no experience at all standing in front of an audience and those who may have had experience with public speaking but did not feel that their previous efforts yielded the kind of results they expected. Because the book was geared initially towards helping people for whom English is not a first language, it was necessary to break down concepts into easily digestible chunks. Native speakers who have used this book have also found this approach useful.

Public speaking students can benefit most if they participate actively in speaking activities. For use of this book in a group class, one of the most effective approaches has been for the facilitator to assign each of the students in the class one section, a full unit, or part of a unit, to review, either in class, or as homework, and to have the student present the information in front of the class.

With this approach, you do not have an instructor lecturing to the participants. Rather, each participant, for a few minutes, gets the chance to deliver a speech in front of peers and the facilitator. Also, participants should be encouraged to give feedback to one another right from the beginning. This affirms that their opinions, feelings, and reactions to others' speeches are valid and worth sharing.

The role of the facilitator will be to model for the participants more effective ways of communicating but only when it is absolutely necessary. Students should be doing most of the talking in the class. At the beginning, of course, the insights of the facilitator will be useful, but if the class is being run well, soon, the participants will be running the whole show.

The facilitator can then provide clarification, as needed, and cheer participants on where spirits may be sagging.

The full range of speaking challenges are covered, from impromptu speaking through extemporaneous to prepared speeches for which one may have several days, weeks, or months to prepare. One of the biggest challenges facing would-be public speakers, however, is how to prepare a speech when time is pressing. This book provides techniques that can help you shine even when you have had as little as five minutes to make your way to the podium.

The confidence that comes from being able to deliver a well-organized speech, when it most counts, is a priceless one. If you have ever been struck by the paralyzing fear of being in front of an audience, you know that the benefit of being able to overcome such a fear is an incalculable one.

Let this book be your companion on what might turn out to be an exhilarating journey. The next page has a model schedule designed for a group of four students and a facilitator, someone with more experience who acts as a guide or coach for the learners.

It can be useful for those who desire to form their own small public speaking practice-group.

Model Public Speaking Class: Facilitator and Four or Five Learners

Some individuals have become great public speakers based on the strength of their determination to become better speakers and on their willingness to practice for long hours in front of a mirror. A good example is Winston Churchill. While it is possible for a solitary, but determined individual to excel as a public speaker, it is probably going to be so much more fun for one to learn with others. By sharing with readers one context (i.e., a small group) in which this book has been used, it is hoped that readers can derive greater benefit from its use.

Class may include:

A Facilitator

Student 1

Student 2

Student 3

Student 4

Model Lesson Schedule for a Two-Hour Class

8:00	Class begins / Greetings / Small talk
8:05-08	Facilitator assigns one unit or a part of a unit to each student to review and prepare notes for a speech in front of the group.

*After the preparation, students take turns in front of the class and share what they have learned.

For example, the Facilitator might assign the following:

Student 1	Unit 1
Student 2	Unit 2
Student 3	Unit 3
Student 4	Unit 4

8:08 – 8:20	Students quietly prepare. About five minutes into the preparation, the facilitator walks around, "visiting" with each student briefly to find out if any one needs help.
8:20 – 8:25	Student 1 delivers his or her speech.
8:25 – 8:28	Students 2, 3, and 4, evaluate Student 1's speech one after the other.
8:28 – 8:32	Facilitator evaluates speaker 1's presentation.
8:32 – 8:35	Student 2 explains his or her assigned unit in front of the class.
8:35 – 8:38	Students 3, 4, and 1 evaluate Student 2's presentation.
8:38 – 8:40	Facilitator evaluates Student 2's presentation.
8:40 – 8:43	Student 3 explains his or her assigned unit in front of the class.
8:43 – 8:45	Students 4, 1, 2 evaluate Student 3's presentation.
8:45 – 8:47	Facilitator evaluates Student 3's presentation.
8:47 – 9:00	Student 4 explains his or her assigned unit in front of the class.
9:00 – 9:03	Students 1, 2, and 3 evaluate Student 4's presentation.
9:03 – 9:05	Facilitator evaluates Student 4's presentation.
9:05 – 9:10	BREAK

9:10 – 9:25   Impromptu Speaking Practice

Each student writes a topic on a small slip of paper (table topic).   Each one folds his or her paper in half.

Students 4 and 2 exchange slips of paper but do not look at what is written on the paper they have received.

Students 1 and 3 exchange slips of paper.

Student 4 stands in front of the class, opens up the slip of paper and announces the topic. Student 4 then has to speak on the topic in question for 1 ½ to 2 minutes.

After the presentation, the facilitator announces the time taken by Student 4. The challenge is to speak for a minimum of one minute and a half and a maximum of two and a half minutes.

Students 3, 2, and 1 give some feedback to Student 4.

The other students take turns giving impromptu speeches, which are then evaluated by their peers and the facilitator.

9:25 – 9:40   The facilitator provides each student with a short article (a different one for each student) cut from a newspaper or magazine. Each student has to present the contents of the article to the class. Rather than just reciting the contents, each student is encouraged to express an opinion on the subject of the article and to add an arresting introduction and a pertinent conclusion. After 15 minutes of quiet preparation in which the facilitator is available to explain words or difficult concepts, the students are ready to present.

9:40 – 9:55   Students present one after the other. After each presentation, the facilitator makes a few brief comments as evaluation.

9:55 – 10:00   Each student is given an opportunity to say a few closing words, which might pertain to their experience of the class or any other thing they want to share with the others. The facilitator thanks the participants and dismisses the class.

Homework might involve getting students to do the exercises on the Fun Spot pages.

Homework might also involve getting students to prepare speeches based on passages taken from other public speaking books, or indeed, their own experiences.

Fun Spot 1: Commonly Confused Words

1	Accede	
2	Exceed	
3	Accept	
4	Except	
5	Access	
6	Excess	

Research

	Term	Definition
1	Acronym	
2	After-dinner speech	
3	Analogy	
4	Bibliography	
5	Demographics	

Notes:

_____
_____
_____
_____
_____
_____

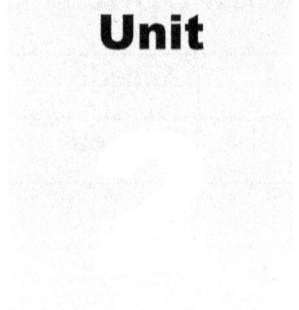

Impromptu Speech
Organizing Framework 1: PPF

If you were sitting comfortably on a sofa at a party where everyone spoke your native language, and someone asked you what your hobbies were, you would have no problem sharing this information and perhaps telling a few interesting stories connected with it. If you were standing in front of a large audience and were asked the same question, how well you do might depend on how much experience you have had being in front of audiences. To be sure, there are some individuals who come across as "natural" even though they may not have had a lot of training. There are individuals who can dance like the Carnival Queen even without the benefit of any special training.

This training manual is primarily geared towards those who recognize that they could benefit from systematic training, even if they are not necessarily starting out as complete beginners.

Some non-native speakers of English imagine that if only English were their first language, public speaking would be easy for them. But speaking in your native language is certainly no guarantee that you will automatically excel as a public speaker. The fear of public speaking is near universal and the fear is apt to bubble up whether you are speaking in your mother tongue, Urdu, Spanish, Putonghua, or English or whether you are speaking in what may be your second, third, fourth, or fifth language!

Certainly, an individual who has to make a speech in a language other than his or her own will have more than one thing to worry about. In addition to ensuring that the content is well organized and makes sense, there is the added worry about grammar, vocabulary, tense, and pronunciation, to name a few.

For any public speaker, having a rough outline in mind as a guide can be helpful. The pressure on you will ease a bit if you have an easy-to-use framework to rely upon. One such framework is structuring your comments with time order in mind. We can always think back to events in the past; we know what is happening around us now, that is, in recent weeks, months or years; and we can also try to speculate about the future.

Let's begin with the first easy-to-apply technique: PPF.

PPF – Past, Present, Future

Let's say your topic is: My hobby

Using PPF you might say something like this:

In the past, I was really keen on playing table tennis. I used to play everyday after school with my siblings and I loved the game so much that one day I remember declaring that I would never stop playing it. I also played for my high school and really enjoyed the friendship and camaraderie among the players – and die-hard fans.

At present, however, I would not even know where to find a table tennis board. I am always so busy that it is difficult to spare any time for such a luxury. The one hobby, however, that I can continue to indulge in is reading. I usually read until I fall asleep, and considering that I hardly ever fall asleep before 3 a.m., you can bet that I am able to get a fair bit of reading done every night.

In the future, though, I plan to be more active. I am seriously considering joining a gym, that is, if I can find one that is on a pay-as-you go basis. I envy my friends who are able to go to the gym about three or four times a week. If I say I want to spend time in the gym, what I am really trying to say is that I look forward to taking up bodybuilding as a hobby.

PPF is generally used to talk about how a situation, perception, or viewpoint, might have changed over time. In some cases, it might focus on evolution, that is, small changes over time. If the changes over time have been dramatic, maybe, calling the whole experience a revolution will be more in order. Essentially, we use PPF to first take a look back to the past, reflect on how the past may be connected to present circumstances, and then, cast our minds to what might happen in the future.

When you are speaking in public, and you have no plan, you might find yourself rambling or to avoid getting yourself in trouble, you might clam up. Some people have literally felt sick upon realizing that all eyes are on them at a time when they do not have a plan to make a coherent speech.

The ideal, of course, would be to calmly present your points, one after the other, and conclude on a powerful note. Having a framework around which to build your comments can provide you with the initial burst of confidence you need to calmly present your points.

A framework provides you with a roadmap. It is up to you to let your knowledge, education, and experience, lead your audience on a smooth ride, with scenic views, the occasional unexpected but totally enjoyable detour, and finally, to a destination that is enthralling, provocative, or simply satisfying.

Here's another example:

What do you think about the world energy situation?

Well, in the past, it was no big deal to build another coal-fired power station if you needed more energy. In those days everything was done in a quick and dirty fashion. This was the situation in the UK one hundred years ago.

At present, this is what's happening in the People's Republic of China. The problem is that the energy situation has changed drastically. Now people have realized that burning coal in the atmosphere is making the climate less stable and life more risky for everyone and everything on the planet.

So, in the future I think we will see coal fired power stations being made illegal in some parts of the world. I think that wind turbines and solar panels, which don't change the environment, will inevitably replace coal.

Here's yet another example on the subject of the Prime Minister of some country.

What do you think about the Prime Minister?

Well I used to think that he was a very capable man and that he would make good decisions for the country.

Recently however, I've changed my opinion. It is clear that he is very indecisive and that this is damaging the country.

I will not be unhappy to see him lose his job in the next general election, which is 6 months from now.

Though you can consciously use the words "past," "present," and "future," you may use other words that signal these time differences as well. In the above example, "I used to" clearly relates to the past, "Recently," is used to signal what is happening currently, and "I will not be unhappy" points to the future.

Consider the example below:

In the past, supplies of uranium for power generation were sufficient to meet demand. In recent years, the supply of uranium to the world market has risen because of increased Russian exports of uranium. These supplies, as you might know, came from nuclear weapons. However exports of Russian uranium are decreasing as all the weapon uranium has been used up.

Now, we are faced with the possibility of a shortfall in the supply and with that, increased prices.

To meet demand for uranium fuel <u>in the future</u> we will need to invest in new sources of uranium, preferably in politically stable nations. If we do not invest now we could have problems obtaining uranium fuel at affordable prices in the future. Additionally, if we do not sign long-term contracts <u>in the near future</u> we could find ourselves buying fuel from less politically stable countries.

One way to look at PPF is simply to remember that it uses time as the organizing framework. This is called "chronological organization". *Chronos* was the Greek God of Time and chronology refers to something being "in order of time."

PPF Practice Topics

1. Reading
2. Getting together with friends
3. Cooking
4. Marriage
5. Women rising
6. Technology
7. Sports
8. Environmental protection
9. Entertainment
10. Eco-tourism

Fun Spot 2: Public Speaking Terminology

Research:

	Term	Definition
1	Body language	
2	Briefing	
3	Bulleted list	
4	Central idea	
5	Chart	

Notes:

_____
_____
_____
_____
_____
_____
_____
_____
_____
_____
_____
_____
_____
_____
_____

Unit 3

Speech Organizing Framework 2: PREP

The method under consideration in this unit, PREP, involves making a strong <u>point</u> to begin with, expanding upon it by giving <u>reasons</u> or justifications, following these with an <u>example</u> or story, and then, rounding it up with a <u>final point</u>. This final point may be as simple as repeating the point made earlier, perhaps doing so in words other than what you had used earlier. The examples that you provide might include personal experiences, case studies, stories, anecdotes, or statistics.

P – POINT
R – REASON (JUSTIFICATION)
E – EXAMPLES
P – POINT

The final point is critical because some people talk and talk and talk and forget what they are talking about. By including the final point, you ensure that your listener knows that you have come to a conclusion. The final point is also a signal for the speaker to not speak endlessly, and either lose the audience or the key message he or she wishes to impart.

Let's say your topic is something as simple as <u>living abroad</u>.

Using PREP, you first make a point. For example, I would love to live abroad, and then, follow it up with a reason. Here goes:

I would love to live abroad. **[Point]**

This is because living abroad is one of the best ways to expand my worldview. **[Reason]**

For example, I know and understand my culture, but I know very little about the worldview of people living in other lands. I have often been surprised that many of my friends from other parts of the world, hold views that differ considerably from my own. I do not believe that any one culture holds a monopoly on wisdom, so living in another culture can help me appreciate new ways of looking at issues and discovering some of the ways in which we can build bridges of friendship around the world despite differences in culture or upbringing. **[Example]**

I am still young so I feel that there is an opportunity for me to expand my thinking and to learn to open my heart to what is unfamiliar. I believe that I can best achieve this goal by spending some time living abroad. **[Point]**

Other words you can use to introduce an example:

Indeed…

Just imagine…

For instance…

Say…

Let's say…

Perhaps…

Maybe…

Consider the following…

Let me share a story with you…

You might be interested in hearing this example…

A story I heard a couple of months ago will illustrate the point…

In the following example, notice the flexibility in applying PREP. You can bring similar flexibility to the use of the other frameworks. Don't become a hostage to any framework. Let it serve as a guideline from which you can exercise your own creativity.

Speaking of a Clean Work Place

The HR department recommends that everyone at Mitsui Bussan Company receive cleaning training. **[Point]**

Why do we recommend this? Well……our research shows that there is a direct relationship between a clean work environment and high employee morale. **[Reason]**

For example, we all know the feeling we get when we go on holiday and we walk into a freshly-cleaned room in a hotel. The sheets are clean, the toilet is sparkling, and the furniture is gleaming. A clean environment makes us feel better. A messy environment makes us feel tired and depressed. **[Example]**

So what's my point? **[Rhetorical question – I'm not expecting anyone to answer me]** *It is simply this. Making our employees feel better about where they work will* *reduce the employee turnover rate.* **[Point]**

Why is this important, you might ask? **[Rhetorical question]**. *Well, Mitsui Bussan Company spends an enormous amount of money and resources training employees. When people leave the company so often we have to spend a lot of time to train new employees. The new employees have less experience and we become less effective as an organization.* **[Reason]**

If we can reduce the employee turnover rate by providing cleaning training to employees we will be able to save money and have a more welcoming workplace. **[Point]**

Topics for Practice

1. Biggest concern for the future
2. Why I love my job
3. Security cameras
4. Children and homework
5. Most influential person in my life
6. The importance of fashion
7. The source of my confidence
8. Learning from life
9. Team sports
10. Solitude

Fun Spot 3: Commonly Confused Words

Research:

	Term	Definition
1	Adapt	
2	Adopt	
3	Affect	
4	Effect	
5	Allude	
6	Elude	

Notes:

_____
_____
_____
_____
_____
_____
_____
_____
_____
_____
_____
_____

Unit 4

Speech Organizing Framework 3: The Six-Finger Speaking Hand

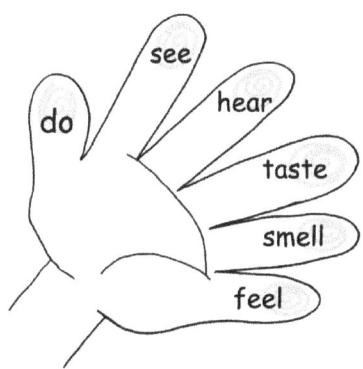

Do – See – Hear – Taste – Smell - Feel

The Six-Finger Speaking Hand technique is particularly useful when one is asked <u>to talk about a place</u>, such as a travel destination. You begin by mentioning why you made the trip. What did you go to <u>DO</u> there? After going through what you <u>saw</u>, what you <u>heard</u> (ocean sounds, bird sounds, the sound of rushing rivers and babbling brooks?), you can talk about the food (<u>taste</u> and the <u>smells</u> (fresh? aromatic? funky?). End by talking about your overall <u>feeling</u>. Would you want to return to that place or is it a place you hope never to visit again?

Model: A Visit to Australia's Gold Coast

Do: *Earlier this year, I went to Australia to attend a symposium organized by my university.*

See: *The first thing that struck me was how small the airport was. I had imagined something rather huge but I was clearly mistaken. I was impressed, however, with the efficiency of the staff. After clearing customs, I did not have to wait long for a bus. In ten minutes, I was in Coolangatta, which was my real destination. As I* *walked around the oceanfront towards my hotel, I could not help but notice how new everything looked. This included the condominiums, homes, cars, and even the trees!*

Hear: *Except for the sound of ocean waves and the gentle breeze, it all seemed so peaceful. There were very few cars so there was no honking of horns. Also, there were not many children. It seemed like a world created for teenage surfers and the happily retired! There were no sounds of temper tantrums. Maybe, things were a little too peaceful.*

Taste: *On my first day, I confess I was not very adventurous, especially when it came to food. I stuck with the familiar fast food fare – I won't mention any names. But then, on the third day, by accident, I came across a burger joint that looked inviting – with so many high-quality magazines spread out for the benefit of clients.*

The burger was made just the way I like it – very well done! Every bite spelled a piece of heaven. I lingered over my meal, read Monocle, and felt like staying there overnight. For the rest of my stay, I made a stop at this burger joint for dinner every night.

Smell: *The air in Coolangatta was as fresh as fresh can be. I spent a great deal of time near the ocean and though I did not surf or swim, just breathing in the fresh sea air, was glorious.*

Feel: *After a week in the Gold Coast area, I decided that this was a place worth coming back to, at least, once a year. It was remarkable that changing the sky over my head, spending a few days in the Gold Coast, brought me such peace of mind. I have already begun to plot details of my next trip.*

Notice that you can talk about things you saw without necessarily using the word "see" or talk about smells without using the word "smell." These elements serve as a mental guide for you and there is no need to be so explicit about them that it becomes apparent you are using a framework. You can even skip some of the elements if they do not seem particularly relevant to the main message you want to convey.

Topics for Practice

1. A trip to the countryside
2. A visit to a former classmate
3. Face to face with my kindergarten teacher
4. My favorite city
5. A place I would rather never visit again
6. A visit to a foreign country
7. The holiday of a lifetime
8. My tropical paradise dream
9. A true travel tale

Fun Spot 4: Public Speaking Terminology

Research:

	Term	Definition
1	Chronological order	
2	Commemorative speech	
3	Concept	
4	Credibility	
5	Credit	

Notes:

_____
_____
_____
_____
_____
_____
_____
_____
_____
_____
_____
_____

Unit 5

Speech Organizing Framework 4: IFONI

IFONI
I – Individual
F – Family
O – Organization (school, business, church, etc.)
N – Nation (government)
I – International

Let's say your topic is pollution and you're living in a city that is heavily polluted. You can talk about how pollution affects some <u>individuals</u>, some <u>families</u>, and include the role of <u>organizations</u> such as businesses in the territory's pollution problem. You can talk about how the <u>nation</u> (government) is making an effort (or not) to combat pollution. Regarding the <u>international</u> aspect, you could talk about intergovernmental cooperation in controlling pollution.

IFONI

Model: Space Travel.

Individual: *Many children dream of going to space. I freely confess that there was a time when I too, dreamed of going to space. But I don't think it was a dream that I took all that seriously. However, when I was living in Hong Kong, I met a remarkable young boy who was applying to join NASA's junior space program and boy did he impress me. I was supposed to prepare him for a selection interview. Though unsure what to expect, I came up with as many as 100 possible questions he might face at the interview. I thought I had questions to work through for several weeks. I was mistaken.*

Family: *On the first day I met the young boy, Brian, who was with his mother. The mother sat at the back of the classroom looking on so that Brian would not be nervous. He certainly was not. He answered all questions with both breadth and depth. Occasionally, Brian's mother would ask me if Brian's answer was good. Most of his answers were right on point. I was able to provide him with some* *pointers that I hoped would make him make an even better impression. As impressed as I was with Brian, I could not help but notice that his mother knew that she had a real treasure on her hands with that special little boy.*

Organization: *Brian explained that he was being sponsored by an organization in Hong Kong that was hoping that in the future, someone from the territory would join NASA in their space explorations. He had already had the opportunity to visit the United States on several space-related camping trips sponsored by that organization but if he passed the upcoming interview he would have a real chance to be a part of the NASA program. I could not help but admire the organization behind Brian, supporting a young boy in his quest for a dream that could also bring glory to his hometown of Hong Kong.*

Nation: *It is remarkable that the United States has made it a matter of policy to include other countries in their space program. It is one of the biggest acts of generosity in the world because the dream of going to space is one that is shared by many people around the world.*

International: *Through international cooperation, the world might draw closer not only in the name of peace but also for the purpose of exploring space so that we can learn more about our place in the universe.*

Topics for Practice

1. Leadership
2. Fun
3. Festivals
4. Building bridges of friendship
5. Saving the environment
6. Goals
7. Winter
8. Olympic Games
9. Pride
10. Automobiles
11. Luxury goods
12. Sports
13. Marathon
14. Keeping wild animals as pets

Fun Spot 5: Commonly Confused Words

Research:

	Term	Definition
1	Allusion	
2	Illusion	
3	Amend	
4	Emend	
5	Anti-social	
6	Unsocial	

Notes:

_____
_____
_____
_____
_____
_____
_____
_____
_____
_____
_____
_____

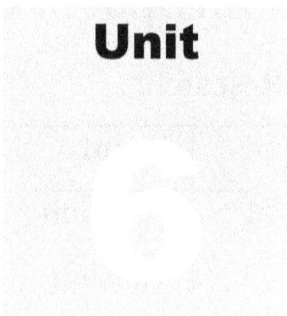

Speech Organizing Framework 5: The Two-handed Mouth

In using the Two-handed Mouth technique, you talk about the two sides of an issue: the advantages and disadvantages, the pros and cons, the good and the bad.

For example, if your topic is Japan, you could have a lot of wonderful things to say about the country, and you could also touch on a few things that irk you.

In all cases, provide examples; tell a story or two, if possible. When stories come out of your own experiences or those of your friends, they are especially easy to tell.

Also, reading a lot can help arm you with a ready supply of anecdotes and stories to call upon when giving a speech.

Model: Playing Golf

Introduction *Golf has captured the imagination of the world in the last few years. Golf tournaments such as the Masters attract hundreds of spectators. It is almost impossible to turn on the television or pick up a newspaper without seeing some* *item of interest on golf. I think that golf has to be seen through two different lenses: one positive and one otherwise.*

Pros — *Golf is great because it is one popular avenue by which business people can relax. After working long hours all week, it must be a great relief to find oneself on a golf course, surrounded by the soothing sights of greenery. The act of hitting the little golf ball can ease stress, and walking on the links in magnificent surroundings must be certainly good for the soul.*

Pros — *Golf is also wonderful in that it can allow people to forge stronger relationships. In the office or in everyday business situations, people hardly ever have the time to talk about things that truly matter. On the golf course, however, one feels free to ask about a business partner's family and to probe a little more into what makes the person tick. Through an exchange of information, and sharing long walks on the golf course, it is possible for a relationship to grow stronger among people who may have been mere acquaintances.*

Cons — *Playing golf, in most places, does not come cheap. As such, it seems that only a certain class of people get to enjoy this fabulous game. The world is trying to bridge gaps among people. In the world of golf, however, money still makes a big difference. Those with access to wealth can better afford the equipment and club fees.*

Conclusion — *Still, a person who is truly determined to enter the world of golf will probably not let lack of money stop him or her.*

Two-handed Mouth: Useful Connecting Words for Comparing and Contrasting

Comparison	Contrast
Like…	On the one hand…
Likewise…	But on the other hand…
Similarly…	The advantage of this…
As…	The disadvantage is that…
At the same time…	Whereas…
As well as…	On the other hand…
In comparison…	In contrast…
Both…	However…
All…	But…
By the same token…	In spite of…
Furthermore…	Conversely…
Just as…	Despite…
Comparable…	Nevertheless…
	On the contrary…
	Instead…
	Rather…
	Notwithstanding…
	Though…
	Yet…
	Regardless…
	Although…
	Unlike…
	Even though…

Topics for Practice

1. Action movies
2. Fast food
3. The Internet
4. Fishing
5. Beauty pageants
6. Bicycles
7. Freelance
8. Dating
9. Dressing well
10. Meetings

Fun Spot 6: Public Speaking Terminology

Research:

	Term	Definition
1	Criteria	
2	Critique	
3	Critical thinking	
4	Filler words	
5	Cultural sensitivity	

Notes:

_____
_____
_____
_____
_____
_____
_____
_____
_____
_____
_____
_____
_____
_____

Fun Spot 6: Public Speaking Terminology

Unit 7

Purpose of the Speech

Establishing the purpose of your speech is very important. The following are some common speech types: Narrative, Demonstrative, Informative, Persuasive, and Humorous.

Narrative: In the narrative speech, you tell a story. Perhaps, you traveled to Australia and had a number of interesting experiences. Your listeners want to know about these experiences and so, you tell them the story. You may have had some humorous experiences and some difficult moments. Through such elements as gestures, vocal variety, and the careful use of pausing, for example, you bring your experiences alive for the audience, along with whatever highs and lows or lessons and insights might be gleaned from the account.

Demonstrative: You may be the representative of a company that has created a new gadget. Your listeners want to know all about it. Using a sample of the product or model, you explain the features of the product and its benefits. You may have to answer questions in order to clarify matters that audience members do not quite follow. If you have anticipated questions that listeners are likely to ask, however, you can craft your presentation to cover all the relevant areas and thus save both yourself and the audience time. Once again, knowing the level of knowledge possessed by your audience will help you tailor the speech to their needs and thus make it both relevant and effective. Demonstration of a new cell phone to telecommunications engineers is unlikely to be the same as explaining new cell phone features to an elementary school class.

Informative: As the name suggests, with this kind of speech, you provide information to your listeners. Your listeners may want to know about how to start a business, how to fly a plane, or how to travel efficiently across Europe on a tight budget. This kind of speech can easily bog down in details. The presenter has to be selective, and know the difference between what is important and what is not. How much time is allotted for the speech, needless to say, can determine the level of detail one can cover.

Persuasive: Your goal in a persuasive speech may be to get your listeners to come to a new way of thinking on an issue. This means that you have to give your listeners good <u>reasons</u> to change their minds. Presenting facts alone, however, does not always succeed in changing people's minds. Like it or not, human beings are emotional creatures and expressing your <u>emotions</u> in a way that comes across as genuine can go a long way towards getting your listeners moved enough to shift their thinking on an issue.

Humorous: Can you make people laugh? The demands of a humorous speech are very simple: make your audience members laugh. Nothing could be clearer. You can combine storytelling, jokes, or one-liners to get your point across. Like any other speech, preparation is essential. Know your audience and the occasion, and factor these into your preparation. Be sure that the time, place, and people are all right for humorous delivery otherwise walking from the podium to your seat may seem like one long unfunny moment in your life.

Fun Spot 7: Commonly Confused Words

Research:

	Term	Definition
1	Artist	
2	Artiste	
3	Ascent	
4	Assent	
5	Assure	
6	Ensure	

Notes:

_____
_____
_____
_____
_____
_____
_____
_____
_____
_____
_____

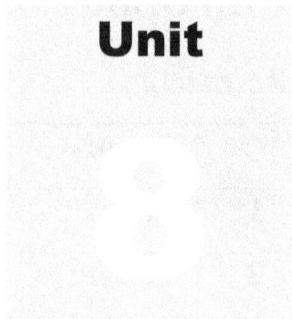

Key Elements for Public Speaking

Public speakers forever need to keep in mind the basic elements of good public speaking. Even though, for the most part, these elements sound simple, they are very easy to forget, especially when under pressure. As such, continual review is necessary to ensure that they become internalized. If you are new to public speaking, the following are the key elements you want to focus on initially.

Good organization: *Introduction, Body, and Conclusion*

Body language: Gestures can enhance a speech. They give your audience an indication that you are truly alive!

Vocal variety: The voice can be a powerful instrument when properly used. Speaking in a monotone is one sure way to put audience members to sleep. Varying the pitch of the voice, raising the voice to make a strong point, and lowering the voice at strategic points can help speakers keep the audience actively engaged in listening.

Pausing/Pacing: The careful use of pausing can help create suspense or anticipation. A speech that goes on and on without any pauses is tiring for audience members. Also, confident speakers are not afraid to pause. If you have something worthwhile to say, the audience will not mind hanging in there with you in those short intervals when you catch your breath or create anticipation before making a critical point.

Do not let nervousness dictate the pace at which you present your material. Breathe in deeply at the beginning. Get a grip on yourself. Remember that your listeners want you to succeed as much as you want to succeed yourself. This is reason for a buoyant spirit, not one of dejection.

Eye contact: A speaker can engage with an audience effectively by maintaining good eye contact. A speaker who looks up or down repeatedly or never makes eye contact with the audience easily becomes disconnected from the audience. Although audience members may make an effort to listen, they may also find themselves tuning out. By looking at different members of the audience for a few seconds at a time the speaker not only signals his or her own sense of comfort as a speaker but also connects with the audience in a way that makes the presentation a shared experience.

Fun Spot 8: Public Speaking Terminology

Research:

	Term	Definition
1	Connective	
2	Definition	
3	Denotation	
4	Dialect	
5	Dyad	

Notes:

_____
_____
_____
_____
_____
_____
_____
_____
_____
_____
_____
_____
_____

Unit 9

Common Public Speaking Problems

Knowing the kind of errors speakers often make in public is one step towards ensuring that you do not make some of the same mistakes.

From the list of common public speaking problems listed on the next page, find out which may be your weakest point. Make a plan, and work on the element of concern until it is no longer a problem. Once you have overcome one problem, focus on a new "weak point" and do everything you can to overcome that as well. Such a concerted effort at wrestling down problems you may have with public speaking can help you go from a speaker with dozens of worries to one with few, if any, public speaking issues to worry about.

On the next page, see a list of common problems.

Common Public Speaking Problems

Introduction not arresting enough	Speaker does not establish authority/ reason why he or she is qualified to speak on the subject	Pacing is too fast
Title and speech do not seem to match	Speech is too short / substance of speech is not clear	Pacing is too slow
Speaker appears distracted and confused	Speaker has too many distracting movements	Poor appearance/ sloppy dressing/ clothing style does not fit occasion
Speaker cannot be heard/voice too low	No facial expressions to indicate emotion	Too tied to notes
Speaker makes no eye contact	Speech content does not match emotion (e.g., smiling & talking about someone's death)	Style is too stilted, i.e., not conversational enough
Speaker makes eye contact with only one section of the room	Props not used properly	Speaker does not pause/speaks so fast that listeners cannot follow
Speech is not well organized/no signposting to guide listeners	Clear lack of preparation/forgetting parts of the speech	Speaker pauses for so long that listeners begin to feel uncomfortable
Speaker appears frozen / no body language	Nervousness too obvious/Shaky hands/ Wobbly knees	No sense of connection with the audience
Speaker stares at one person for too long, making the person uncomfortable	Poor grammar	Conclusion has no spark

Which of the Common Public Speaking Problems noted on the previous page would you consider your biggest weaknesses now?

Fun Spot 9: Commonly Confused Words

Research:

	Term	Definition
1	Aural	
2	Oral	
3	Berth	
4	Birth	
5	Bloc	
6	Block	

Notes:

_____
_____
_____
_____
_____
_____
_____
_____
_____
_____
_____

Fun Spot 9: Commonly Confused Words

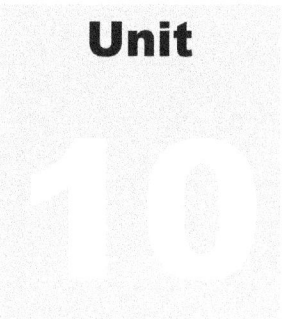

Unit 10

Positive Elements in Public Speaking

Some of the positive elements pertaining to public speaking that you will do well to keep in mind are on the next page. These can serve as targets for constant review.

As with the common public speaking problems presented earlier, decide on which of the elements you most want to focus on. Pour your energies into improving these elements and then, once you have made enough progress on one or a couple, begin to focus on other elements.

If you persist in doing this over time, you will make steady progress and eventually achieve the goal you have set for yourself.

Guaranteed Formula for Public Speaking

Positive Elements:

Introduction attracts attention	Speaker tells story engagingly
Voice is clear	Speaker uses expressive voice/vocal variety
Volume is sufficient	Speaker is creative
Speaker uses signposting/Gives preview of what is to come	Points are easy to follow
Choice of vocabulary/diction fitting for the occasion	Speaker uses colorful language
Introduction/Body/Conclusion	Humor is tastefully used
Speech is logical	Topic fits interest of audience
Audiovisual materials effectively used	Speaker is not tied to his/her notes
Speaker appears confident and poised	Speaker uses conversational style
Speaker makes eye contact across the room	Speaker uses repetition to reinforce point
Pacing of the speech is perfect	Speaker signposts the conclusion/listeners have an indication conclusion is coming
Information is engaging/stimulating	Speaker makes good use of transitions
Speaker's approach is original	Speaker is balanced/not dogmatic
Speaker is energetic/dynamic	Main points are supported with examples, anecdotes, quotes, statistics, etc.
Speaker establishes rapport with listeners	Main points are clear

Positive Elements You Want to Focus on Now

Guaranteed Formula for Public Speaking

Fun Spot 10: Public Speaking Terminology

Research:

	Term	Definition
1	Ethos	
2	Ethnocentrism	
3	Eulogy	
4	Evidence	
5	Extemporaneous speech	

Notes:

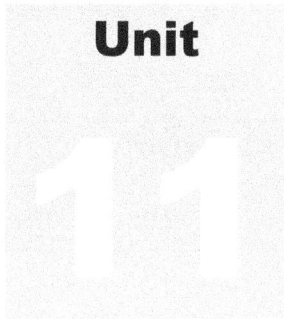

Know Your Audience

The kind of speech you give often depends on the kind of audience you have. In other words, even when you have the same material, it is unlikely that you will be able to give the exact performance between varying audiences. And this should not be your goal anyway. After all, different audiences have different characteristics and energy levels.

Giving a speech to a group of business executives is unlikely to be the same as giving a speech to elementary school students even if the topic is the same. This means that you have to adjust your introduction, possibly your examples, and other elements of your content, to suit the audience. Therefore, the more you know about the audience the better.

For example, you will not talk about the New York subway system to someone living in the Big Apple[1] in the same way you would to a person who just landed there. This means that you need to be aware, to some extent, of the knowledge level of your audience. This will help you avoid spending too much time on things that your audience members know (and thus putting them to sleep) and rather, concentrate on what may be new and stimulating information for them.

---

[1] Big Apple = nickname for New York City

Fun Spot 11: Commonly Confused Words

Research:

	Term	Definition
1	Blond	
2	Blonde	
3	Born	
4	Borne	
5	Brake	
6	Break	

Notes:

_____
_____
_____
_____
_____
_____
_____
_____
_____
_____
_____

Fun Spot 11: Commonly Confused Words

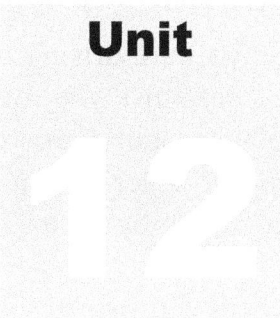

Unit 12

Good Organization: Introduction, Body, and Conclusion

Focus on Introductions:

It is important for a speech to have an introduction, a body, and a conclusion. The introduction sets the background for the speech and prepares audience members for what is to come. A popular recommendation regarding speechmaking goes like this:

> Tell 'em what you are going to tell them **(introduction)**;
> tell them **(body)**; and
> tell them what you told 'em **(conclusion)**

At the very least, the introduction should set the stage for the presentation: why should the listeners be interested in the topic? Does the topic affect their lives or those of their children? Is there a crisis that is connected in some way to their lives or is there some benefit they can expect? Lay down the reason why this speech is important to the audience and give them a road map as to what they can expect in the speech. For example, on a speech on the environment, here's a possible introduction that includes background, the relevance of the speech to the audience, and what the body entails.

Model 1: *Ladies and gentlemen. Thank you for coming, especially on such a night as this when the rain is coming down in sheets. I am sure you will all agree that it is impossible these days to turn on the TV or read the newspaper or even walk down the street without being reminded that we are killing the environment. You think of yourself as a concerned citizen, someone who would like to contribute to a better world but feel that you do not know how to make a real difference and help prevent a global catastrophe in the near future. Well, I'm going to present three concrete ways through which you can make a difference. These include, first, following the 3 R's (reduce, reuse, recycle) in your daily life; second, supporting neighborhood programs and last, connecting with global organizations that focus on environmental protection.*

Signposting

When you are driving in an unfamiliar city, you appreciate seeing clear signs along the way. These give you the assurance that you are moving in the right direction. Some of the signs might warn you against turning onto a certain road. Others will bring you a feeling of relief as you realize that soon, you will arrive at a spot where you can have a hearty lunch or get to use the restroom.

Speakers can provide such signposts for their listeners as well. When listeners have a mental outline of the speech, they can determine roughly where they are at any given time. Often, when speeches drag on too long, the expression, "In conclusion," brings a sense of sweet silent relief to the audience! That is an example of a signpost, but you do not have to wait until you are near to the end of the speech before you give such signals.

After you have connected with your audience by means of a joke, a scene-setter, or an anecdote, you can give the audience an idea of where you are all headed. Let them know what key points you are going to cover and how many. Don't keep this a secret. Audience members will be happy to go on the intellectual, humorous, informative, or inspirational journey with you if they have an idea of where you are headed together.

Model 2: *There's an old saying, "Travel and see." Ever since I heard that saying, I have been traveling as much as I can to find out how much I can see. Today, I am going to share with you some of my bungee jumping adventures and what I have learned along the way. <u>First, I will share with you some background information on bungee jumping</u>, including its origins; <u>then I will highlight the top bungee-jumping spots</u> around the world; and <u>finally, I will tell you about my experience of bungee jumping with Queen Nio'Alonoa in Hawaii.</u>*

Fun Spot 12: Public Speaking Terminology

Research:

	Term	Definition
1	Eye Contact	
2	Fair use	
3	Fallacy	
4	Feedback	
5	Figurative expression	

Notes:

_____
_____
_____
_____
_____
_____
_____
_____
_____
_____
_____
_____
_____

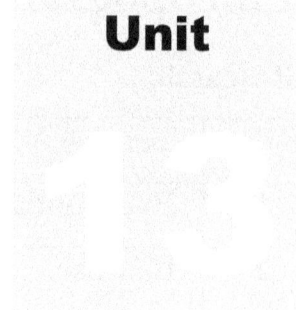

Quick Introductions

A good introduction paints a picture for audience members before launching into the meat of the topic. You want your introduction to grab the attention of the audience but this certainly does not mean shouting for attention. A shocking statement, quietly made, can be just as powerful as one uttered at the top of one's lungs.

Some people find it difficult to come up with an introduction to a speech. Some spend hours, days, even weeks coming up with an introduction. In some cases, there might be much sighing, moaning, groaning, and perhaps a touch of regret for having accepted to give the speech.

If you are going to give a speech to a large group and have several years' advance notice, and you spend weeks and weeks trying to come up with the best introduction, you can be duly excused. That's what presidents and prime ministers do, or if truth be told, that's what presidential speechwriters are paid to worry about. However, if you have been asked to give an overview of your company's marketing program at a meeting that is about to start in ten minutes, you do not have the luxury of procrastinating over your introductory comments.

Quick Intro is a technique that makes it easy for you to come up with an introduction to practically any topic under the sun. It does not require paper, pen, pencil, pad, iPad or iPod. All you need is your mental apparatus and a willingness to tap into your knowledge and experience. With practice, you will never have to waste precious time agonizing over how to craft an introduction that is both engaging and pertinent.

We all have an idea of what people in our community think about various topics. That general idea can be a great resource for preparing introductions. Sometimes, we agree with the common view; sometimes, we disagree. This common view can be the starting point for introducing your topic.

By reflecting back to the audience what the common perception about an issue might be in their community, you start the speech on a gentle, non-threatening note. This is likely to be something that audience members are familiar with. Some might agree with this general viewpoint. Naturally, others might not. But that is not the point. The point is that you need to start somewhere.

The next step is to give an example or two to make what you are saying crystal clear to the audience. Then, state your own position on the matter. Your own point of view may either agree or disagree with the general view. Whatever it is, if you can come up with three points to support your point of view, you have the basis for a full speech. All you need to do then is expand each of the three points with some examples, stories, and anecdotes.

Let's see how this works in practice.

Quick Intro
Most people think……………………………………………………………………..

For example……………………………………………………………………………

I think……………………………………………………………………………………..

Let's say your topic is Sumo Wrestling.

Model:

> *Most people think that sumo reflects how such an advanced nation as Japan is still very much steeped in tradition.*
>
> *For example, sumo wrestlers are required to perform various rituals such as the throwing of salt in the ring. The meanings of such rituals are not clear to many people.*
>
> *I think that sumo wrestling has much to teach the world about holding on to traditional values. I am going to explain three ways by which some of these traditions can enrich the world beyond the borders of Japan. They are 1) highlighting respect for the past, 2) inculcating discipline among children, and 3) teaching the idea of responsibility early in life.*

If you mention your three points, you will be giving your listeners a road map or **signpost** about what they can expect. You can use "because" to signal the introduction of your three points.

For example,

> *I think that robots will help save the world **because** 1) they can do all the dirty work that humans do not like to do, 2) they can replicate themselves, and 3) they do not need to be fed*

Guaranteed Formula for Public Speaking

If your viewpoint differs from the general view you can signal this difference in opinion by using "Although" as a starting sign. For example,

> ***Although*** many people think that robots are the future, I think that robots are dangerous for the following reasons: 1) they steal jobs from people, 2) they have no feelings, and 3) they have the potential to replicate themselves

Once some speakers latch on to **Quick Intro** they never want to let go. Rather than always using "Most people think….," however, try other variations such as the following:

- There is a common perception that…
- In general……………………….
- A widely held notion is that………
- It is commonly thought that…
- It is often said that….

Quick Intros can be fun. Knowing that you can create an instant introduction for practically any topic is liberating indeed.

Topics for Practice
Create a brief introduction for each of the following topics without writing anything down. Create your introduction mentally. All you need are about five or six sentences.

1) New Year's resolutions

2) Protecting wildlife

3) Monasteries

4) Penguins

5) Pirates (on the ocean)

6) Piracy (of intellectual property)

7) Internet search engines

8) Sunscreen

9) Wine

10) Personal freedom

Fun Spot 13: Commonly Confused Words

Research:

	Term	Definition
1	Bridal	
2	Bridle	
3	Brooch	
4	Broach	
5	Canon	
6	Cannon	

Notes:

_____
_____
_____
_____
_____
_____
_____
_____
_____
_____
_____
_____

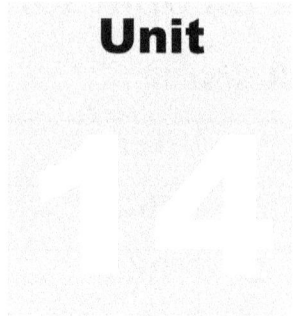

Notes: To Use or Not to Use

To the extent possible, please avoid writing down your speech, especially when you do not have a lot of time to prepare. If you write down the speech, you will likely find yourself reading it. Such a speech is unlikely to be viewed as a great speech.

Rather, as a timeless piece of advice from ancient Roman, Quintus Horatius Flaccus highlights,

> *Seek not for words, only fact and thought*
> *And crowding in will come the words unsought*

It is easier to make a speech from points (a list of key words and phrases) than beginning public speakers often suppose. Some want the safety of complete sentences, fearing that they will not be able to fill in the blanks if they depend on memory joggers (key words and phrases) alone.

Written speeches have their place in very formal settings and occasions. Abraham Lincoln is said to have labored over the Gettysburg Address, writing and rewriting it until it became the perfect gem that we know it to be. But did he simply read it to the assembled crowd? Reading any written speech requires skill if the speaker is to simultaneously connect with the audience.

Let's find out how easy it is to make a speech from points. It requires some thought, to be sure. But once you have found the thread that connects all the individual points, you do not need the crutch of relying on long written-out sentences. Each point will call to mind the idea you want to express. Link your ideas together with some transition expressions, and you have the makings of a speech!

Assume that the points below were jotted down yourself for a speech. Without writing anything else down, create a story or speech around these points. You already know how to use Quick Intro, so be prepared to start with an introduction.

Think about this for two minutes and try to give a 2-3 minute speech. If you can include a few stories, present a few details about some of some of the characters, and use a bit of creativity, this should not be too difficult.

Try it.   Notes for a speech)
- last year/visit
- hometown/friends/family
- fun – activities/food
- connections
- next year/plans

The danger of memorizing word for word

Word for word memorization poses a danger. If you forget one word, you could find yourself standing in front of the audience unable to proceed as you try to recall that one forgotten word. The pause soon stretches beyond what might be considered normal and people begin to wonder if you have forgotten part of your speech. Soon, you are in a panic. You apologize.

This can be avoided, however, by practicing a speech in a way that gives primacy to ideas rather than words. Even if a particular word is forgotten, the thought can be completed using other words that convey the same meaning.

A simple way to be mentally prepared for any potential public speaking situation is to tell yourself, "If I am asked to speak about subject X, FIRST, I will talk about A, then I will touch on B, and finally, I will cover C." With this simple outline in mind, you are already in the starting blocks. With this rough outline in mind, connected to a subject you know well, you are in a far better position to respond to any speaking requests than someone who has not given any thought to the possibility of getting called and suddenly hears her name or his name!

Memory Aids

Already, we have learned about PPF, PREP, and IFONI, and how they can act as frameworks for talking about various issues. While you do not want to memorize everything in your speech word for word, you can use acronyms to aid your memory when you have to present a list of items. For example, in opening a public speaking workshop, the chairperson had to make some brief comments after calling the meeting to order. These included explaining that evaluation forms were available, reminding audience members about the timing rules for impromptu and prepared speeches, and finally, introducing the special guests.

By using ETI as a memory aid, the chairperson was able to go to the lectern without any notes and to talk about <u>E</u>valuation, <u>T</u>iming rules, and do the <u>I</u>ntroduction of special guests. The chairperson already knew all this information but was worried about mixing them up. By using ETI as a framework it was easy to proceed smoothly. Let's say, in your speech, you want to give a number of fruits as examples. Here is your list: Elderberry, Coconut, Guava, Banana, Avocado, Date. Is it easy for you to remember them? Compare the above with the following list in alphabetical order: Avocado, Banana, Coconut, Date, Elderberry, and Guava.

Which is easier to remember?

Research using Articles, Essays, Stories, and News Reports

Beginners at public speaking who find it difficult to write speeches or take too long in doing so can benefit from the use of short articles found in newspapers, magazines, newsletters, and the like. The ideas presented in an article can be the starting point for exploring your own thinking.

For practice, you may summarize the points made in one or several articles, making sure to use your own words. Rather than just summarizing the article, you can also indicate to what extent you agree or disagree with the writer. You can then advance your own points to give a more balanced picture of the information in the article. Of course, credit should be given to the source of your information.

To get a balanced view of any subject it is much better to use not just one article but rather, several. Also, keep in mind that there are many speeches that can spring from the speaker's own experiences and therefore require minimal use of outside sources. Seeking opportunities to make different kinds of speeches — storytelling, public relations presentations, sales, or motivation, and others can help you grow both in your style of delivery and in mastery of content organization.

Fun Spot 14: Public Speaking Terminology

Research:

	Term	Definition
1	Gestures	
2	Groupthink	
3	Hidden agenda	
4	Lectern	
5	Main motion	

Notes:

_____
_____
_____
_____
_____
_____
_____
_____
_____
_____
_____
_____
_____
_____

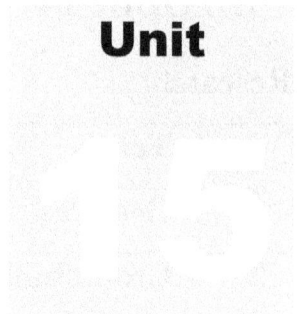

Introduction to Speech Evaluation

Evaluation is the lifeblood of any effort to improve one's public speaking abilities. Public speaking students would do well to learn how to evaluate others as this helps them to become more aware of what they themselves need to improve.

Evaluation should not be thought of as mere criticism, however. Effective evaluation ought to come from a higher plane, a place of wisdom and care and concern for the speaker. Some like to distinguish between "constructive criticism" and "destructive criticism" but as the word criticism itself carries a negative connotation, why not use the term *evaluation* rather than *criticism* when weighing the success of a particular speech.

Evaluation of a speech involves looking for the good points, the strengths of the speaker as well as those areas that can be improved. As a speaker, it is important not to be too defensive about evaluations. The evaluation is the evaluator's subjective view and may or may not be right. There are times when you, as an evaluator, will think that you have given a very considerate, fair, and helpful feedback to the speaker but in the speaker's mind you could not have been more insensitive.

In the end, the speaker can decide what to accept and what to reject. If you are a speaker, however, and every evaluator is telling you that because of how fast you speak, your message may not be sinking in for audiences, you might infer that there is something of value in that point.

When people work together to improve their public speaking skills, they have a better chance of achieving their goals, particularly if they are willing to honestly evaluate one another. However, honestly evaluating others does not mean condemning any and everything that may seem less than perfect in your eyes.

In a group, therefore, it is important for members to watch out for one another. When an evaluation of a particular speaker seems too harsh, others might want to highlight some of the better qualities and speech elements of the speaker under fire, to bring some balance to the atmosphere and to avoid discouraging the recipient of the overly harsh criticism. It is important to strike the right balance between "criticism" and "encouragement." With practice, however, each individual can become a master evaluator and learn to provide the kind of honest feedback that recognizes the strengths of the speaker while also pointing out areas that can be improved.

A good evaluator is like a wise friend who is interested in the welfare of the speaker and so speaks with pleasure about the speaker's strengths and with kindness, empathy, and understanding about the areas that could be improved.

Tact is in order at all times.

But Me No Buts

Evaluators would do well to banish the use of the word "but" from their vocabulary when introducing an area for improvement. This is because "but" negates any positive feelings you might have established at the beginning of the evaluation. It takes practice to avoid using "but." You will, find, however, that your evaluations will be much better received if you do not use the deflating connective, "but," to signal the beginning of your comments about what needs to be improved.

Consider the following:

> *Mr. Rogers did a good job of introducing his topic <u>but</u> his content was very confusing.*

Rather than introducing the negative element, "but," why not consider a pause or introduce some other transition words or phrases.

For example,

   a) *Mr. Rogers did a good job of introducing his topic. With much clearer organization of his material, he could have more easily reached the hearts and minds of the audience members.*

   b) *Mr. Rogers did a good job of introducing his topic. I wondered if he could have had a greater impact by mentioning at the outset the order in which he was going to handle the main points.*

Notice that in the two examples above, there was no use of "but" even though there was a shift from focusing on positive elements to points of growth. Sometimes, all you need is a pause to signal a transition from one set of ideas to another.

Guaranteed Formula for Public Speaking

We all know that no speech is perfect, so try to avoid the habit of always harping upon this simple fact. Instead of:

> *Mr. Rogers gave a wonderful speech. I liked it very much, <u>but as we all know no speech is perfect</u>, so I am going to mention some of his weak points….*

Try something like the following:

> *Mr. Rogers gave a wonderful speech. I liked it very much, in particular his use of gestures to emphasize key points. When he talked about the globe I thought he had another opportunity for a big, emphatic gesture. That would really have made his points stronger.*

Fun Spot 15: Commonly Confused Words

Research:

	Term	Definition
1	Canvas	
2	Canvass	
3	Cast	
4	Caste	
5	Censor	
6	Censure	

Notes:

_____
_____
_____
_____
_____
_____
_____
_____
_____
_____
_____
_____
_____

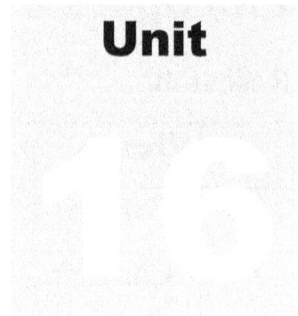

The Sandwich Technique for Speech Evaluation

The sandwich technique offers a tactful way of sharing your opinion about a speaker's performance without destroying the speaker's confidence.

The use of the sandwich technique encourages you, the evaluator, to be broad-minded, observant, honest and generous at the same time.

Using the sandwich technique, even before hearing a speech, the evaluator acknowledges that no speech is entirely bad or entirely good. This allows the evaluator to watch out for both positive elements, for example, the speaker's proper use of eye contact and gestures, and areas for improvement, such as the need for more vocal variety.

Also, an evaluation is the evaluator's subjective view and experience of the speech, so it is not a good idea to present it as the final word. As such, instead of saying, "You should look up more," you would probably be better off saying something like, "You might want to look up more."

When you say someone should do something, it seems as though you are the only voice of authority; however, when you say that a person might want to consider doing something, you acknowledge that the individual in question has the power to decide. It is also much more respectful and a speaker who is asked to consider something is much more likely to heed the advice than one who has been commanded to do it!

Not surprisingly, there are three parts to the sandwich technique.

         Positive points   -   **Points of growth**   -   **Positive points**

Positive points: Tell the speaker what you liked about the presentation. Did you become more informed as a result of the speech? Did the speaker maintain eye contact? Did he or she make good use of the voice? Referring to the key elements for public speaking (introduction, message, gestures, eye contact, pausing/pacing, conclusion, etc.) can be a starting point to help you know what to comment on.

Points of growth: What could the speaker have done better? Would the speech have worked better if the speaker had spoken in a louder voice? Were you able to follow the speaker's argument? Letting the speaker know what might have been improved, along with possible suggestions on how to do so, could be useful here. Some say that there is no perfect speech and that it should always be possible to find at least one point the speaker could improve. This places some pressure upon evaluators to observe the speaker and listen conscientiously.

If you say a speaker has given a perfect speech when this is, in fact, not the case, you have not been of help to that speaker. In your lifetime, however, you may hear a speech that seems perfect in every way. When you find yourself observing such a phenomenon, do not shrink from saying that you have seen a touch of the divine. Rare as such cases may be, if you ferret out problems that did not exist, you are the one who will seem out of place and out of touch. On the other hand, if everyone thinks a speech is perfect, and you are still able to find a genuine point of growth for the speaker, your star rises. You gain respect.

Do your evaluations with a generous heart and be truly concerned about helping the speaker and you cannot go wrong.

Positive points: You do not want to leave your hardworking speaker deflated, so conclude with another positive point. This might be an expression of your overall feeling towards the performance of the speaker. *(I thought you were very courageous to tackle a topic like that and to maintain eye contact with practically everyone in the room. Good job!)*

Don't Kick a Person Who is Down

As a student of public speaking, you will have occasion to see some wonderful performances in your lifetime. You will also, almost certainly see, one or two people at low points in their lives: the speaker who leaves the podium halfway through what seemed like a marvelous speech, the speaker who forgets lines that had been learned with assiduity and is inconsolable, the speaker whose nervousness is palpable from the shaking knees and fluttering hands and bobbing head. You might also have occasion to encounter the utterly unprepared and wonder why the person had not simply canceled his or her participation.

If you are the evaluator for any such individuals, you might be tempted to be stern and to sharpen your tongue for a verbal 'whupping': *"Why didn't you take the time to prepare?" "Couldn't you have taken a few minutes to check your slides?"* Please don't.

The speaker you aim to chastise is not unaware of the immense personal failure. Such a person may be in mental agony and is unlikely to benefit from being overloaded with virulent criticism. Go lightly.

In such instances, the effectiveness of your evaluation will be in the empathy and kindness and consideration that you show to a person who is so obviously in trouble.

Fun Spot 16: Public Speaking Terminology

Research:

	Term	Definition
1	Manuscript speech	
2	Maxim	
3	Message	
4	Monotone	
5	Non-sequitur	

Notes:

_____
_____
_____
_____
_____
_____
_____
_____
_____
_____
_____
_____
_____

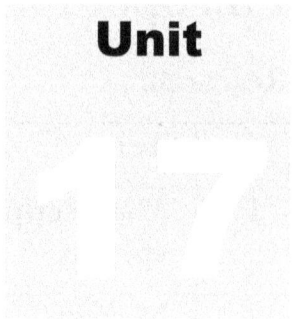

Sandwich Technique Template

The following template can provide the reminder one needs to focus not only on areas that need improvement but also on the speaker's strong points. Sandwiching the areas of improvement between positive comments is a practice that is useful not only for evaluating speakers but also in providing feedback in many areas of life, whether to friends, family, or colleagues.

Positive point:

Point of growth:

Positive point:

Fun Spot 17: Commonly Confused Words

Research:

	Term	Definition
1	Childish	
2	Childlike	
3	Complement	
4	Compliment	
5	Continual	
6	Continuous	

Notes:

_____
_____
_____
_____
_____
_____
_____
_____
_____
_____
_____
_____

Unit

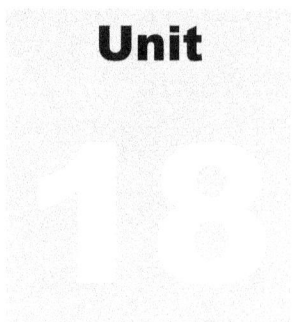

The Speech Burger / Write Burger

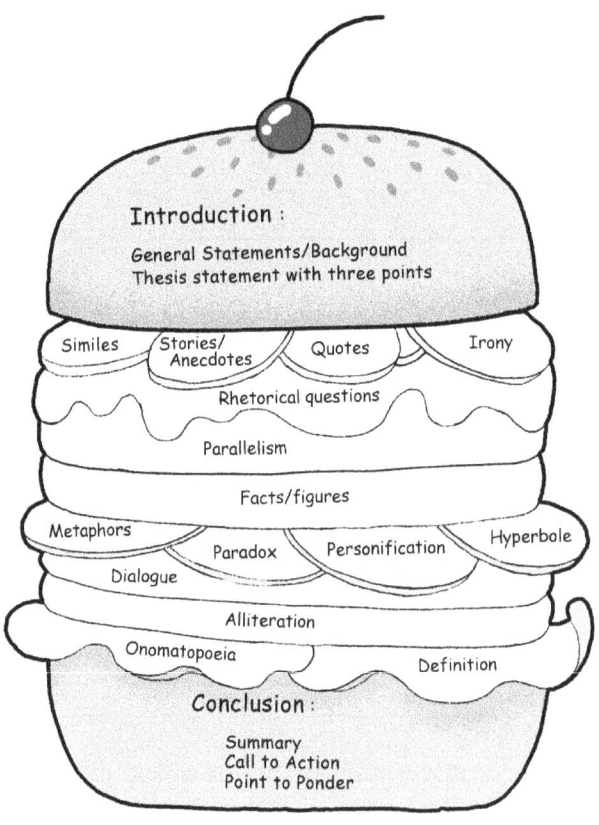

Just as a burger requires the top and bottom buns, a speech needs an introduction and a conclusion. In the case of a burger, as important as the top and bottom buns are, they are not enough to make the burger the tasty treat that it is expected to be.

As such, just as you need your cheese and your lettuce and your tomatoes and your mayonnaise to create a tasty burger, you need anecdotes, rhetorical questions, similes, irony, dialogue, etc., to craft a great speech. You may not need all these elements in every speech. Without any such elements, however, your speech is likely to lack spark.

Unit 21 takes a closer look at the ingredients in the speech burger.

Fun Spot 18: Public Speaking Terminology

Research:

	Term	Definition
1	Red herring	
2	Reliability	
3	Speech outline	
4	Stage fright	
5	Sub-points	

Notes:

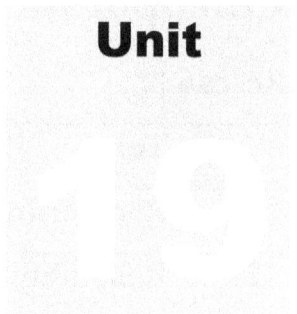

How to Write a Speech…If You Must

As a speaker, you do not want to build your fame on being the kind of person who always reads speeches. But there are times when it does not hurt to write a speech. When Dr. Martin Luther King Jr. decided do speak out against the Vietnam war, he knew that his stance was an unpopular one and that it was important to lay out his argument very carefully. He enlisted some of his most trusted associates to help him draft the speech. Dr. Vincent Harding, a professor and writer, and a friend and colleague of Dr. King, is credited with having written the first draft of what became the "Beyond Vietnam" speech at New York's Riverside Church on 4 April 1967.

But writing a speech does not mean that you must read it like a bedtime story. You can practice so well that the delivery is not stilted and mechanical.

Despite the attention to speech crafting by Martin Luther King Jr., his lawyer and friend, Clarence Jones, who also drafted speeches for the preacher, notes that Dr. King was a master at mentally "copying and pasting" speeches that he had given before. This means that a good speaker has to be nimble. To ensure that a particular speech fits the audience, time, and place, there are times when you have to deviate from what you had planned.

As a speaker, it does not hurt, as part of your preparation, to jot down ideas and to give physical form to the speech in the form of a written text. The text might change considerably over time, meaning that what you begin with may end up being completely different from what you deliver. Still, the discipline of writing can be useful. When you have delivered hundreds of speeches, it might occur to you that you can do without preparing speeches that are too rigorously focused on words. After all, with key ideas in mind, you should be able to call upon words at will to express the ideas you have in mind. Therefore, the following, rather than being injunctions to be obeyed to the letter, may be considered more as guidelines for serious consideration.

In the end, however, your goal should be to find what works for you. If you find that you can work out speeches in your mind without having to write anything down, you are ahead of the game. Others might find that try as they might they cannot create speeches without writing down their thoughts in sentences. Also, there are special occasions where one's speech must be presented in writing first, perhaps to the media, before delivery. In such cases, you do not have much of a choice but to write a well-crafted speech. Read and practice such speeches aloud so that you can have a feel for how they will sound when delivered.

Know Your Objective

Are you trying to inform, persuade, or entertain?

Find a Title

Some people find a title first and write a speech to fit the title. Others may have something to say and find a title to fit what they have to say. In any case, be sure that by the time you're done, you have a title. This will be needed to give you a fitting introduction and it will make you come across as well prepared, and your ideas focused.

It does not seem professional to have the one introducing you say to the audience,

> *"Ladies and gentlemen. We're very happy to have Ms. Akiko Tang Young with us today. She is going to say something related to the ocean and the rivers and water in general but she does not have a title so relax and take it all in."*

One of America's foremost writers, Gay Talese, notes that he often writes his books before giving them a title. To him, the broad theme is important but capturing the essence of his book in a few words has often been the work of his editors. For you, as well, it may be possible that getting the best title is not your strongest suit. Don't let this hold you back. Focus on getting your message down as clearly as possible. Sometimes, in the course of preparing the speech, the best title will occur to you. Sometimes, the title will occur to you after the speech is all done. Keep thinking about it but do not let the lack of a title hold you back from starting your preparation.

Do Research

Speeches that give evidence of research can be very powerful. A speech that is peppered with quotations, statistics, anecdotes, etc., can give the impression that the speaker cares about the subject and by extension, the audience. It can also give the impression that the speaker is smart, passionate about facts, and meticulous.

Be aware, however, that too many facts and statistics can weigh a speech down and suck the life out of it. By all means, use facts and figures but don't drown your audience in them. The connections you make among a few well-chosen facts may have far more of an impact than stringing together facts, figures, and factoids one kilometer long.

Write It Out?

In some cases, such as when dealing with a highly technical speech or when you have a lot of time or when your life depends on it, it may be a good idea to write out everything. Then read it aloud. At this point, some parts may not sound right. Make necessary changes. Add more facts if necessary; remove what does not seem to fit. This may take time, which is why it is a good idea to start working on your speech as soon as possible. Don't wait. Time flies!

With practice, however, you'll come to appreciate the value of using an outline rather than writing down everything. Using point form (key words and phrases) and practicing your speech aloud, making changes here and there, allows you to know your speech intimately and makes you more flexible, which can be important when you have to cut down your speech. Written speeches often come across as stiff. If you want your speech to have a natural tone, try speaking it out first, perhaps in chunks, and getting them down on paper. Pay attention to how the words sound and you will be able to prepare a speech that is pleasant for audience members to hear.

The Rule of Three

Don't cram your presentation with too many points. If you can highlight three main points, you're doing well. Each of these points may be supported by examples, quotations, anecdotes, or other pertinent comments to make them crystal clear. Present too many points, and your audience may find it difficult to remember anything you said!

Fun Spot 19: Commonly Confused Words

Research:

	Term	Definition
1	Cord	
2	Chord	
3	Corps	
4	Corpse	
5	Council	
6	Counsel	

Notes:

_____
_____
_____
_____
_____
_____
_____
_____
_____
_____
_____
_____

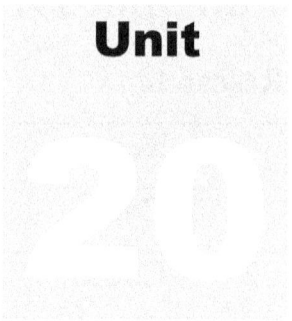

Five Ways to Begin Your Speech

Depending on what your speech is about, you can decide on how best to grab the attention of the audience. If you give a lot of speeches, it is a good idea to vary your openings. You do not want to be too predictable. At the same time, it is important to keep in mind what the purpose of the introduction is: to seize the attention of the audience and keep it throughout the remainder of the speech. Here are a number of ways you might choose to begin your speech, besides using the Quick Intro technique.

1) Start with a startling fact

> *One out of every four people you see on the street will die early because of smoking!*

2) Start with an anecdote

> *I was pedaling my bicycle one early morning…it was quiet and I was finally glad that I was getting in shape…I was full of excitement about what lay ahead…there were no cars on the road, no people, and so I rode faster and faster…when I raised my head I realized I was heading straight for…*

3) Start with a quotation

> *The Dutch artist Vincent Van Gogh said, "I put my heart and my soul into my work, and have lost my mind in the process."*

4) Start with a rhetorical question

When you ask a rhetorical question, you do not expect your listeners to answer the question; you just want them to think about it.

> *Ladies and gentlemen, let me begin with a question for you. How would it be if the oceans of the world rose by only five inches every year?*

5) Start by <u>setting a scene</u>

Get the audience to imagine a particular scene. Supply them with the elements necessary such as tone, key words, a story, and get them in the mood for your presentation.

> *Imagine yourself on an island; you are there with someone you truly care about…your initial impression of the island was that it was a tropical haven…but you have discovered to your dismay that there is no water there. Everyone has left and the two of you are alone…*

Fun Spot 20: Public Speaking Terminology

Research:

	Term	Definition
1	Target Audience	
2	Testimony	
3	Toast	
4	Verbatim	
5	Visualize	
6	Word Whiskers	

Notes:

_____
_____
_____
_____
_____
_____
_____
_____
_____
_____
_____
_____
_____

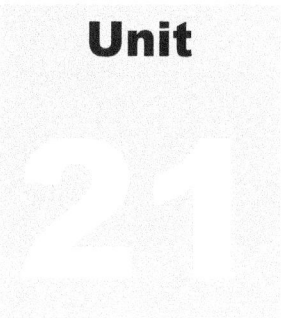

Unit 21

The Speech Burger – A Closer Look

Have you ever been at one of those functions where you hear a speech, maybe a long speech, and yet moments after leaving the auditorium, you could not remember anything from the speech? If you have had such an experience, don't blame yourself alone. The speaker has to share the blame. Good content, well prepared, has to be combined with superb delivery to make a speech memorable.

The following devices can help add pizzazz to your presentations; they are the reason some speeches have become unforgettable to us. Use them to make yours memorable as well.

Body:

Stories/anecdotes: A short story that makes a point can help support the overall theme of your presentation.

> *When I first came to Japan in 2002, I attended a Japanese language school in Iidabashi, an area in Tokyo. One day, after class, I was in a rush to go meet a friend. At the train station, I put a 10,000 yen bill in the ticket machine; out popped my ticket. I grabbed it and rushed through the turnstile and onto a departing train. As soon as the door of the train shut, I realized that I had not picked up my change. At the next stop, I got off and made my way back to Iidabashi. Needless to say, the money was not there.*
>
> *Visions of starvation floated through my mind. But then I went over to the station attendant and, in halting Japanese, explained what I had done, how foolish I had been. A sly smile passed the lips of the attendant. He pulled out a brown envelope from a drawer and handed it to me. That moment, for me, crystallized the reality of honesty in everyday Japanese life.*
>
> *Now, let's see by a show of hands how many people have heard similar stories or experienced similar acts of honesty in Japan?*

Similes: When you say that A is <u>like</u> B you are making use of simile.

My girlfriend is <u>like</u> a tiger!

He ran as fast <u>as</u> the Maglev train.

Metaphors: A metaphor is <u>not unlike</u> a simile, except that instead of using like or as, it is direct, more like an equation: A = B.

My girlfriend <u>is</u> a tiger. She is always ready to pounce at the least misstep on my part.

Quotes: Hillary Clinton, after losing the 2008 Democratic nomination to Barack Obama, said, with women in mind:

Although we weren't able to shatter that highest, hardest glass ceiling this time, thanks to you, it's got about 18 million cracks in it. And the light is shining through like never before, filling us all with the hope and the sure knowledge that the path will be a little easier next time.

Irony: A rather simplistic definition of irony is when you say the opposite of what you truly mean. For example, you say:

Sumo wrestlers are too puny. They need to eat more!

Or it's raining and you say, *"What great weather, eh?"*

Here's how one online dictionary explains irony: "the use of words to convey a meaning that is <u>the opposite</u> of its literal meaning: the irony of her reply, "How nice!" when I said I had to work all weekend." (Source: http://dictionary.reference.com/browse/irony)

Rhetorical questions: In this case, you ask a question without really expecting an answer? You may supply the answer later on in your presentation. The point is that you do not pause for the purpose of getting an answer from the audience. Your pause may simply be to get them to think about the question.

Are we going to do nothing while our jobs evaporate? Are we going to sit down and just hope for a better tomorrow instead of planning for a better day? Are we so content with our suffering that we feel no need to act?

Facts/figures:

Every three seconds a child dies somewhere in the world because of malnutrition.

Personification: Personification is when you give non-humans or inanimate objects the characteristics and traits of a human being.

- *The rain water galloped after the little kids.*
- *The moon smiled upon the river bank.*
- *The clock wailed at noon.*

Paradox: According to the Merriam Webster dictionary (www.merriam-webster.com), paradox is "a statement that is seemingly contradictory or opposed to common sense and yet is perhaps true." Here are two examples of paradox from Merriam Webster:

It is a paradox that computers need maintenance so often, since they are meant to save people time.

As an actor, he's a paradox—he loves being in the public eye but also deeply values and protects his privacy.

Hyperbole[2]: This is exaggeration to the extreme.

My uncle is so tall he can scratch the sky.

Dialogue:

Grace said, "We always complain about people in times past who did not do their part to improve the world around them."
Molly replied, "Yes, it's a bit hypocritical of us, isn't it? What have we been doing to make the world a better place? Now, there is global warming, AIDS, hunger, and poverty. We better take action."

Sometimes, recreating dialogue in a presentation can bring both the subject matter and the characters alive for the listeners.

Alliteration: With alliteration, you have a <u>succession of similar consonant sounds</u>. In the above case, you have "s" sound repeated over and over.

<u>A famous alliteration:</u>
Peter Piper picked a peck of pickled pepper, a peck of pickled pepper Peter Piper picked; if Peter Piper picked a peck of pickled pepper, where is the peck of pickled pepper Peter Piper picked?

---

[2] Pronunciation: \hī--pər-bə-(-)lē\

Onomatopoeia: Onomatopoeia refers to words that imitate sounds that they are supposed to represent. Examples include the following: knock, moo, splash, boom, and mumble.

Definition: As a speaker, there are times when you might use words that the audience might not be familiar with. In such cases, it is the course of wisdom to provide a definition. In other cases, a definition might be necessary because of confusion about the meaning of a particular term. The dictionary can be the first step in finding a definition but there may be extended definitions that might help make the word or term even clearer to the audience. Giving concrete examples is one way to extend the definition of a word.

Parallelism: You are using parallelism when you have a similar sentence structure, in pairs or threes…or more.

I came,
I saw,
I conquered.

I have given my life to the fight.
I have given my energies to the challenge.
I have surrendered my spirit to the cause.

While others were sleeping, I was writing.
While others were surfing, I was reading.
While others were eating, I was typing.

Fun Spot 21: Commonly Confused Words

Research:

	Term	Definition
1	Dairy	
2	Diary	
3	Dependant	
4	Dependent	
5	Desert	
6	Dessert	

Notes:

_____
_____
_____
_____
_____
_____
_____
_____
_____
_____
_____
_____
_____

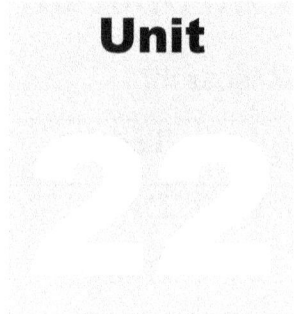

Effective Conclusions

A speech that ends abruptly could leave audiences confused and unsatisfied. A speech may take audiences to dizzying heights. A speech may take audiences to the deepest valleys. A speech may take audiences over high waves and gentle surfs. If you are doing a good job, the audience will ride along with you. However, you have to bring them safely home, not leave them dangling from cliffs or stranded on the high seas. Let your speech answer questions that may be on people's minds. If you made a promise at the beginning, by the end of the speech make sure that you have fulfilled the promise.

When you have to give a speech, give some thought to the kind of conclusion you want to give. Do you want to leave the audience grinning broadly while you make your exit or do you want them to have thick, knotted brows as they ponder the weighty issue you have laid upon them? Do you want your audience to feel that they can go out and achieve their dreams or do you want them to sit silently and think deeply about responsibilities ahead?

Once you determine the kind of effect you want to leave with your audience, you are ready to choose an appropriate method to conclude. There are quite a few to choose from. In the following sample conclusions, imagine the introduction and body already delivered.

A point to ponder: Get your audience to think.

> *If we do nothing about the environment, we may live our lives in peace but another generation may come after us for whom everyday will be a matter of pain. Of course, we would be long gone by then, but our children and grandchildren will wonder how selfish we might have been to leave a dying world for them.*

Action:

One hundred yen will buy you a piece of gum. One hundred yen will buy you a cheeseburger. One hundred yen can also feed a child in a developing nation for one week. Do you have one hundred yen to spare to feed a hungry soul? If so, when we leave here, go to the Internet, go to the Oxfam website, send them a few hundred yen, and be a hero to a child that might have died but for your generosity.

Rhetorical questions:

How do we feel when we see homeless people on the streets? What does it say about our country that we cannot provide shelter for the weak among us? What does it say about our sense of compassion when we refuse to allow the government to build homeless shelters in our neighborhoods?

Summary:

We have learned that in order to succeed, we need to identify exactly what it is that we want; we need to have a plan that is flexible, and that we need to persist until we achieve the goal that we set for ourselves.

Quotation:

…and so, ladies and gentlemen, are we being good neighbors, good friends, good husbands and good wives? Are we helping those around us, or are we hindering their every move? Are we biting the people around us or are we building them up? As the late great beauty and philosopher Marilyn Monroe said, "Dogs never bite me, just humans." With that in mind, go…and bite others…no more!

Dramatic statement:

…when next you enter the hospital, do not forget…please remember… that, "Doctors are the third leading cause of death."

Restate your purpose:

At the beginning of this presentation, I said that working together, we can get the city to take the concerns of ordinary people seriously. If we remain united and press the municipality with our demands, they cannot help but respond. We have the strength of numbers on our side. Politicians love numbers. If they realize that we have a large number of supporters, they cannot help but yield to our demands.

Fun Spot 22: Public Speaking Terminology

Research:

	Term	Definition
1	Rostrum	
2	Pulpit	
3	Dais	
4	Lectern	
5	Podium	

Notes:

___
___
___
___
___
___
___
___
___
___
___
___
___

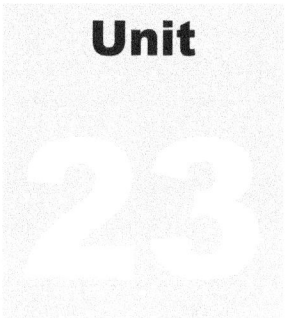

Unit 23

How to Introduce a Speaker

Speech introductions should be treated as mini-speeches, which means that they ought to have a <u>beginning</u>, a <u>middle</u>, and an <u>end</u>. Sounds familiar? An introduction should not be so long that it overshadows the upcoming speaker and his or her speech. At the same time, it should not be so short that it takes away from the importance of the speaker and the speech. Remember that this is an opportunity for the speaker to be introduced to the audience and for the audience to be introduced to the speaker.

A speaker who is made to feel important goes to the stage with the wind on her back, confident, and ready to do the very best. On the other hand, when a speaker is not introduced properly, she carries some feelings of disappointment with her to the stage and if not careful, this could be reflected in her performance.

Introducing a speaker, therefore, should not be taken lightly. It is a responsibility that can either contribute to the success of a speaking engagement or take some of the sheen off it.

Ask yourself:

- What motivated audience members to attend?
- What are the needs of this audience?
- What is the background of the speaker?
- Why is this speaker right for the audience?

Three Steps to Introducing a Speaker

Introduction: Begin by addressing the audience. Make sure that you have the attention of the audience.	*Ladies and gentlemen.*
Middle/Body: Tell the audience about the speaker's qualifications, experience or connection to the topic.	*The issue of global warming continues to worry many of us. but the issues do not appear to be getting any clearer. Dr. Kafka Kakanaka of the International Oceanic Research Institute has devoted most of his life to the study of the issue of global temperature and is going to share some of his insights with us in a speech entitled: <u>Global Warming: Fact or Fiction?</u>.*
Conclusion: Invite the speaker to the lectern. Lead the applause. (Start clapping vigorously!!!)	*Ladies and gentlemen, would you help me welcome our next speaker, Dr. Kafka Kakanaka!*

Fun Spot 23: Commonly Confused Words

Research:

	Term	Definition
1	Discrete	
2	Discreet	
3	Dual	
4	Duel	
5	Eatable	
6	Edible	

Notes:

_____
_____
_____
_____
_____
_____
_____
_____
_____
_____
_____
_____

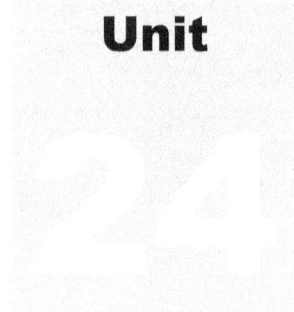

Introducing a Speaker: Preparation Sheet

The following preparation sheet can be useful in allowing you to get all the necessary information to craft an introduction that does justice both to the speaker and the audience.

Name of speaker: _____

Speech title (if any): _____

_____

Why the issue is important to the audience: _____

_____

Why the speaker is qualified to speak on this topic: _____

_____

Convert the written comments above into points (bulleted key words or phrases). Reading your introduction is almost never a good idea. To be sure, there are cases when it might be advisable to do so. Use point form, practice, and if possible, do the final introduction without using your notes (though it does not hurt to have it handy, just in case).

Introduction text – key words and phrases (beginning, middle, end):

_____

_____

_____

_____

_____

_____

(LEAD THE APPLAUSE/START CLAPPING!!!)

Quick Review

- Welcome audience
- Connect with audience by acknowledging their needs
- Highlight the background of the speaker
- Make the connection why this speaker is a good fit for the audience
- Invite audience to welcome speaker (Applause!)

Fun Spot 24: A Word to the Wise

There are always three speeches, for every one you actually gave. The one you practiced, the one you gave, and the one you wish you gave.

~Dale Carnegie

Unit 25

Short-notice Speech Preparation

When you do not have a lot of time to prepare a speech, you can use Quick Intro to get yourself into gear. You will recall that in using Quick Intro, you come up with a few general comments to seize the attention of the audience, give some examples to focus the subject even more, and then follow these up with your thesis or main theme, which you might link to three points you want to cover. Those three points can become the basis for the body of your speech. All you have to do then is expand upon each of the points using examples, stories, statistics, or anecdotes; make some logical connections and you have a speech that is ready for delivery.

Use the Short Notice Speech Preparation template at the end of this unit, to prepare your speech. Create an original introduction that gets your listeners' attention; prepare and deliver the presentation from bulleted key words and phrases rather than sentences.

Your introduction will comprise a few general statements to capture the attention of the audience and a narrower statement that directs their attention to the three main points you want to highlight. The bulk of your time is best spent on coming up with appropriate examples, anecdotes, statistics, and metaphors to back up your three points.

Quick Intro: (General statements + Thesis statement)

General statements: *Most people think that young people ought to get involved in sports.* **After all, sports activities are** *not only good for the development of their bodies but also participation in sports can keep young minds healthy and sharp. But a key question arises. What is the best kind of sports for young people. Is it basketball? Is it soccer? Is it rugby? I think it's none of those.*

Thesis statement: *I think tennis is the best game because*
a)........
b)...... and
c)..........

Expand each of the points, a, b, and c, in the body, add a conclusion and there you have it!

The Short Notice Speech Preparation template at the end of this unit helps you expand upon the Introduction, Body, and Conclusion into 5 parts, with the <u>Body</u> part breaking down further into <u>three paragraphs</u>. But rather than writing down sentences, just focus on the points you want to make. If you have been able to tie three points to your introductory comments, then all you have to do is think about the examples and anecdotes and quotations and explanations and similes and metaphors that go with each particular point. If the examples and stories you use come mostly from your own experience and those of people connected with you, or perhaps, through books you have read, just a word or two can be enough to trigger the memory.

Write the points down as quickly as you can. In 5 minutes or less, you should be able to prepare notes for a speech on a subject you know well.

Using a copy of the Short Notice Speech Preparation Template on the next page, and timing yourself for 5 or 6 minutes, practice preparing notes for the following:

1) Why I love my job
2) Welcome to my hometown
3) City life
4) My first year on the job
5) My favorite hangout
6) Maintaining relationships
7) Communications technology
8) Volunteering
9) The United Nations
10) My favorite childhood toys

Short Notice Speech Preparation Template

Title: _____

Introduction (including 3 points you want to highlight)	
Point 1	
Point 2	
Point 3	
Conclusion	

Fun Spot 25: Commonly Confused Words

Research:

	Term	Definition
1	Effective	
2	Efficient	
3	Elicit	
4	Illicit	
5	Eligible	
6	Illegible	

Notes:

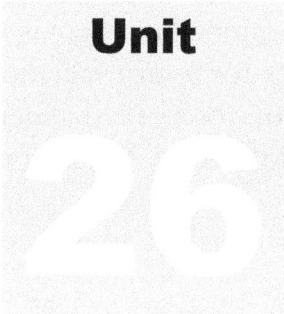

Speech Evaluation: The CR Technique

Earlier on, you learned how to give feedback to speakers using the Sandwich Technique. As important as the sandwich technique is, it is now time to move on and learn about another technique: The CR Technique.

Look at the evaluation of a speech as a mini-speech. This means that we need an introduction, a body, and a conclusion.

CR simply refers to **C**OMMENDATION and **R**ECOMMENDATION.

In the <u>commendation</u> (C) section you compliment the speaker for something he or she did well and <u>give a reason</u> for it.

> *Your use of eye contact was fantastic. You made me feel as if I was the only person in the room and I have the feeling that others felt similarly that you were paying close attention to them. That kind of eye contact is difficult to make but you made it seem so easy. I was very much impressed.*

If you have two points for <u>commendation</u>, all the better. Then you make a <u>recommendation</u> (R) to the speaker and <u>give a reason for it</u>.

> *I would recommend including more pauses. Your words flowed like Niagara, a clear reflection of your passion, energy, and desire to share important information. With more pauses, more of us would have been able to follow the ideas. Before I could digest one great idea, you were already on to an even greater idea…A pause every now and then would definitely have allowed me to ride on right along with you….*

Rather than jumping into the evaluation with your first positive point as the sandwich technique suggests, with the CR technique, you have an opportunity to deliver a real introduction, that is, you set the stage with your own general statements and observations before getting to the evaluation proper.

Likewise, after focusing on specific <u>commendations and their reasons</u>, and <u>recommendations plus reasons</u>, you give a summary or conclusion. If you have prepared notes for your evaluation, both the introduction and conclusion, which ought to come out of your broad general experience, need not be delivered with any notes. You should try to wing it. You will make a better impression.

Let's consider an example.

Model CR Evaluation

Intro:

> *Madam Chairman, ladies and gentlemen, and most especially Ms. Tatiana Ogawa. I'm sure that in recent years you have all wondered about the issue of holiday travel. Ms. Ogawa's choice of topic showed that she is very much in tune with the audience today and I'm sure many of us are going to benefit from the recommendations she made. In any event, I am going to focus on 2 key strengths and one area of growth.*

Commendation (C): Issue + Reason

> *Ms. Ogawa, one of your key strengths has to do with connecting with the audience. When you came on the stage, you did not rush into the speech. You stood comfortably and looked around, as though you were weighing with your eyes all the members of the audience. You gave us the impression that you were interested in all of us, and your question about how many people plan to go back to their hometowns and the time you took to look at the respondents, showed that you were really interested in the audience.*

C: Point + Reason

> *You also established trust. You gave us a reason to trust you. You detailed your qualifications and shared with us how long you have been studying the issue of holiday travel. We felt that you were someone we could trust to have insights about a subject that is of great concern to many in the audience.*

Recommendation (R): Point + Reason

> *You really had the audience in the palm of your hand. You stood right here and still managed to connect with all sides of the room, often just by turning your body to one side or the other. You did that quite effortlessly, which gave me the impression that this is a style that you have perfected over time. I wondered if you could have made greater use of the stage. You could have paced up and down from time to time. This would have added to the effect of authority that you had established at the beginning. Audiences are also attracted to movement so you could have used movement to hold your audience even closer.*

Summary:

I know I am not the only one who will enjoy my journey home this holiday season. Through the use of humor, research, and experience gained over many years, Ms. Ogawa kept us at the edge of our seats as we took in the nuggets of wisdom she had so carefully prepared. I plan on going home and re-planning my summer vacation. If anyone here wants to know how to connect with an audience and speak with the voice of authority, all you have to do is remember Ms. Ogawa's speech today. She connected with us and inspired trust. I can imagine Ms. Ogawa using more of the space on the stage next time. Thank you, Ms. Ogawa for the great gift of your insights, which will serve us all for many years to come.

Madam Chairman.

Speech Evaluation Form: CR Technique

Intro:

Commendation (C): Point + Reason

C: Point + Reason

Recommendation (R): Point + Reason

Summary

Fun Spot 26: A Word to the Wise

Be sincere; be brief; be seated.

~ Franklin D. Roosevelt (on speechmaking)

Unit

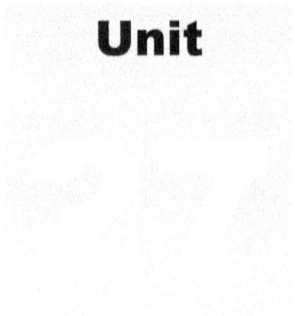

Evaluating the Evaluator

Here is a chance to evaluate a speech evaluation. Let's say you are Person "C." You listen to a speech made by Person "A," along with another Person, "B," who evaluates A's speech. Next, listen to B's evaluation of the speech, and make some notes, using the template on the next page, and give B, the evaluator, some feedback. Which of the evaluator's comments did you think were right on point (well done) and which did you think could have been better presented?

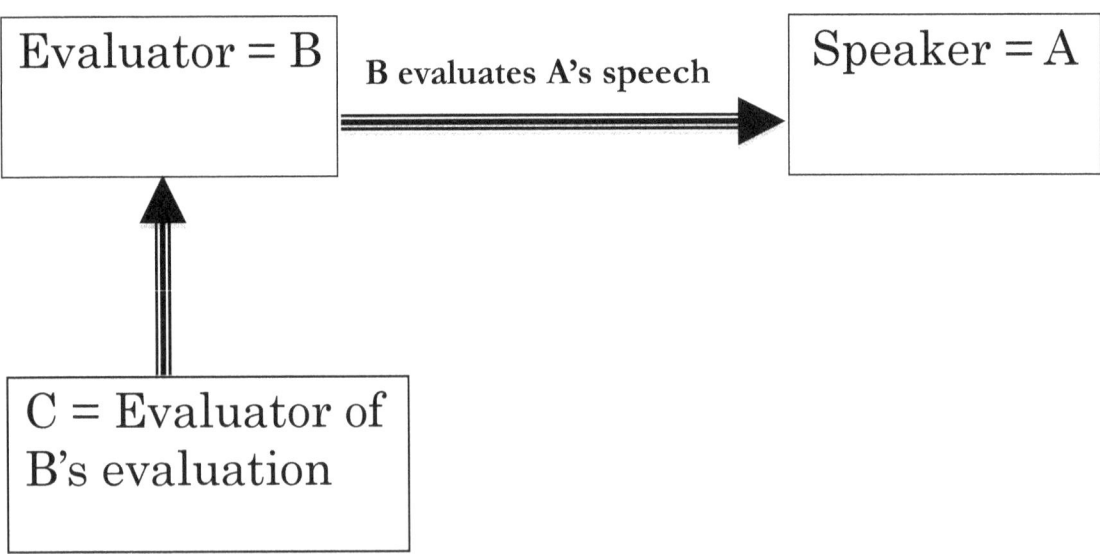

This exercise can help sharpen your awareness about speeches and evaluations, both of which are critical to your development as a communicator.

Evaluating the Evaluator: Template

Evaluator's comment on	Well done?	Could have been better?
1) Clear introduction		
2) Commendations		
3) Reasons for commendations		
4) Recommendation		
5) Encouraging tone		
6) Eye contact		
7) Gestures		
8) Poise/appearance		
9) Clear conclusion		

Guaranteed Formula for Public Speaking

Fun Spot 27: Commonly Confused Words

Research:

	Term	Definition
1	Emigrant	
2	Immigrant	
3	Eminent	
4	Imminent	
5	Ensure	
6	Insure	

Notes:

_____
_____
_____
_____
_____
_____
_____
_____
_____
_____
_____

Fun Spot 27: Commonly Confused Words

Unit 28

For the Mind's Eye: Painting Pictures

As the old Chinese saying goes, "A picture is worth a thousand words." Some of the most memorable speeches throughout history are memorable precisely because they are rich in imagery. Of course, if you're talking about your visit to Bora Bora and you bring along a picture, that would show your listeners a great deal more than you could probably ever describe. Yet we do not always have the luxury of being able to show real pictures to an audience. We can do the next best thing, however, by painting mind pictures for the listeners. In the following example, notice the emphasis on <u>places</u>, an attempt to get people to imagine these places and the fighting that would take place there. Also note the power of the repetition of "We shall fight…"

Winston Churchill:

We shall go on to the end, we shall fight <u>in France,</u>
we shall fight <u>on the seas and oceans</u>,
we shall fight with growing confidence and growing strength <u>in the air</u>, we shall defend <u>OUR ISLAND</u>, whatever the cost may be,
we shall fight <u>on the beaches</u>,
we shall fight <u>on the landing grounds</u>,
we shall fight <u>in the fields and in the streets,</u>
we shall fight <u>in the hills</u>;
we shall never surrender.

IMAGE OF CHANGE – Turning the Page (Note the repetition)

Barack Obama: *…That's how change has always happened – not from the top-down, but from the bottom-up. And that's exactly how you and I will change this country. California, if you want a new kind of politics, <u>it's time to turn the page</u>. If you want an end to the old divisions, and the stale debates, and the score-keeping and the name-calling, <u>it's time to turn the page.</u>*

If you want health care for every American and a world-class education for all our children; if you want energy independence and an end to this war in Iraq; if you believe America is still that last, best hope of Earth, then it's time to turn the page.

It's time to turn the page for hope. It's time to turn the page for justice. It is time to turn the page and write the next chapter in the great American story. Let's begin the work. Let's do this together. Let's turn that page. Thank you.

(From Barack Obama's speech to the California Democratic Convention 2007)

When the Chinese talk about someone having an iron rice bowl, they are referring to a secure job, such as one with the government. You may know someone who is a social butterfly or the rock that you turn to in times of trouble.

As you prepare your speech, consider what images can help crystallize the points you want to make in the minds of your listeners. Churchill, for example, combines metaphors with parallelism, and the repetition of particular phrases.

Still unsure?

According to Tokyo-based public speaking enthusiast and energy industry businessman, Mr. Hitoshi Yasuda, a speech is best conceived of as a song. He notes that just as a song has a lead or hook that draws the audience into it, along with some high points, mellow and powerful parts, as a speaker you are unlikely to hold the attention of the audience members if you deliver the whole speech in monotone. A singer who sang in just one tone might be run off the stage. As a speaker, you cannot afford to hold yourself to a lesser standard. So, pay attention to the "music" of your speech and consider how you will manage the tone, timbre, pitch, volume, and even melody of your presentation.

On the other hand, another businessman, Mr. Seiji Nakura, also based in Tokyo, conceives of a speech as a painting. Paintings that hold our attention such as those by Picasso, Monet, or Van Gogh, have various elements that draw our attention to different parts of the work – a splash of red here, a speck of shade there, a jagged line there. While there are elements in the painting that hold the whole image together, part of the pleasure of looking at a painting is to appreciate how all the different elements blend to create a pleasing image. And so it must be with your speech. Where is the color? Where the shade? Where the line that leads the eye across the canvas? Where the curious blob that gets the viewer to strain her neck?

Like singers and painters who enthrall us with the magic of their gifts, you can also deliver speeches that carry a spark of magic, and thus, inspire, motivate, inform, teach, entertain, persuade…and entice others to reach for the best that is within themselves.

If you want to give speeches that people will remember for many moons to come, pull out your palette of colors and start painting some vivid images for your listeners. Savor the applause.

Exercise:

Prepare a 2-3 minute speech, making use of images to drive your point home.

What kind of images do you associate with the following topics? That is, if you were to give a speech on any of these topics, what images would you create in the minds of your listeners.

- The current state of Planet Earth
- Apparently successful companies that resort to deceptive practices
- Career success
- Margaret Thatcher was described as <u>the iron lady</u>; how would you describe some famous people from your country or culture?
- High cost of education
- Amusement parks
- The ozone layer
- Noise pollution

Fun Spot 28: A Word to the Wise

Always be shorter than anybody dared to hope.

~ Lord Reading (on speechmaking)

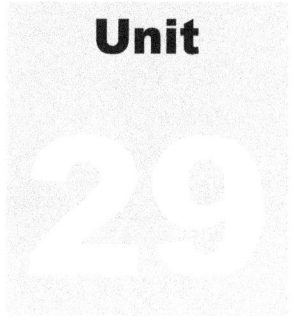

Speech Introductions: Using an Anecdote/Mini-story

In *How to Argue and Win Every Time*, Gerry Spence, an American lawyer who never lost a criminal case in over 40 years of practice, writes:

> *Storytelling has been the principal means by which we have taught one another from the beginning of time. The campfire. The tribal members gathered around with little children peeping from behind the adults. The old man, can you hear his crackling voice, telling his stories of days gone by? Something is learned from the story – the way to surround and kill a saber-toothed tiger, the hunt for the king of the mastodons in a far off valley, how the old man survived the storm. There are stories of love, of the discovery of special magic potions, of the evil of the warring neighboring tribes – all learning of man has been handed down for eons in the form of stories. We are, indeed, creatures of story.*

If storytelling is good enough for Mr. Spence, it's probably good enough for you and me!

Here's an example of using an anecdote to begin a speech

> *A few weeks ago, I went to Australia's Gold Coast. I was really excited about the trip and wanted to go back to the same hostel where I had lodged the last couple of times I went to that area. From the airport, I grabbed a bus and in less than 10 minutes I found myself at the reception desk of my favorite backpackers hostel.*
>
> *"Hello Sir, I would like to check in," I said. "Do you have any beds?"*
> *"Yes," replied the manager, "but you cannot stay here."*
> *"What do you mean I can't stay here?" I asked, baffled.*
> *"This is a backpackers hostel and you are not a backpacker."*
> *"Well, I may not be carrying a backpack but I am travelling more or less like backpackers do."*
> *"What brought you to the Gold Coast?" he asked.*

"I am attending a symposium at one of the local universities."
"Exactly. So, you are not a backpacker."
"But being a student does not mean that I could not be a backpacker. Many backpackers are students."
"Indeed, but at this moment you are not a backpacker, and so we cannot accept you."
"So, if my two bags had been backpacks, would you have accepted me?"
"Of course. We only accept people who are backpacking and are carrying backpacks..."
"This is so unfair," I muttered under my breath as I grabbed my two bags and slinked out of the hostel.
Now, have you ever found yourself in such a nice little pickle overseas? Today, I am going to talk about how to make traveling overseas a joyful experience even when others try to pile up obstacles in your way.

Discussion:

- What introduction styles do you usually find easier to use?
  Question? Quotation? Anecdote?

- How long do you spend preparing your introduction?

- What is your goal in the introduction?

Practice Exercise
Use an anecdote to introduce a speech on any of the following topics:

- Courage
- Fame
- Friendship
- Bullying
- Happiness
- Freedom
- Loss
- Cowardice
- Envy
- Determination
- Serendipity

Fun Spot 29: Commonly Confused Words

Research:

	Term	Definition
1	Epigram	
2	Epitaph	
3	Esteem	
4	Estimate	
5	Flair	
6	Flare	

Notes:

_____
_____
_____
_____
_____
_____
_____
_____
_____
_____
_____
_____
_____

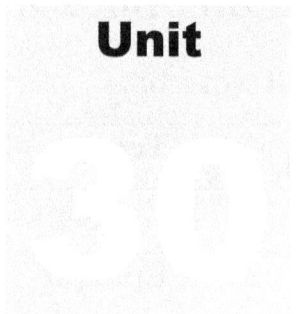

Vocal Variety: Using the Greatest Musical Instrument, the Voice

As a speaker you have a great deal of potential power – the power to move your audience. No matter how brilliantly crafted your speech may be, it is unlikely to affect people if it is delivered in monotone. None of the individuals who are often cited as great speakers spoke in monotone: John F. Kennedy, Barbara Jordan, Martin Luther King Jr.

During the 2008 presidential campaign in the United States, the world saw a number of the candidates display superb public speaking skills. For example, when Hillary Clinton wanted to drive home a point, she would sometimes end her delivery with a rise in her voice. That got audience members excited. Often, it was also a well-timed invitation for applause since the emphasis in her tone was a clear marker of the importance of what she had just said.

The point is that good speakers know when to lower their voice, and when to lift it up in a crescendo of rolling words and tumbling phrases. If you have prepared effectively, you will know which parts of your speech are best delivered in a normal voice and which parts deserve special treatment.

Having some kind of a wave pattern in a speech can allow the audience a period in which they listen to straight or level-tone delivery punctuated by highs and lows. Hopefully, the low points are not too low! Make your speech an adventure of sorts for the audience. Let it have some gentle slopes, a couple of valleys, a plateau or two, and several peaks. At the end, you bring the audience home safe and satisfied.

Unless you are being paid to lull your audience to sleep, please avoid speaking in a lifeless drone!

a) Practice speech:

   You won the scholarship. Oh my. I will miss you. So when are you leaving? Next week? That's too soon, isn't it? It took a while to know that this big dream of yours can come true. You worked hard for it. You should be proud of yourself. But what am I going to do without you here? It's going to be hard on me. But I will be okay. I know I have to be happy for you, and I am. Indeed…from the bottom of my heart.

Read the practice speech above as though your were:

a) ecstatic

b) angry

c) relieved

d) sad

e) being sarcastic

b) Write a paragraph on a subject of your choosing and practice reading it with any of the emotional overtones noted above.

Fun Spot 30: A Word to the Wise

The best way to sound like you know what you're talking about is to know what you're talking about.

~Author Unknown

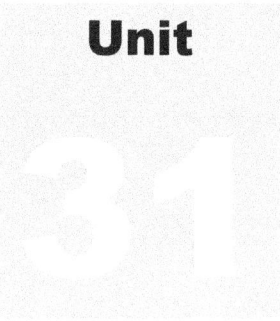

Connecting with the Audience

Some of the members of your audience may have traveled a long way to come and hear you speak. If people have taken the time to come and listen to you, you owe them some respect. They have shown interest in you. Why not show some interest in them? And if people have traveled a long way to come and hear you, you better not look like a scared little kitten behind the lectern. Project a sense of confidence. For that matter, it matters not really, how long or how far people have traveled to come hear you. Any audience is important for being kind enough to lend you their ears.

Confidence begets confidence. If you look confident, the audience will feel that they are in good hands and that they have not wasted their precious time to come and listen to you.

This matter of confidence is of great importance even before you speak. Long before you have taken up the microphone, people will be sizing you up. And how you approach the stage will say volumes about you, even before you have uttered a single word.

A confident bearing (your responsibility) and a good introduction (the MC's responsibility) are a good combination. The introduction, if well done, helps both the audience and the speaker to gain the understanding that the two are going to be good for each other. The audience will judge you as being dynamic, smart and eloquent, or any number of things, even before you have said a single word!

A warm smile and a brisk pace towards the stage will do much to provide the necessary assurance. A speaker who is shaking like a leaf in the wind even before getting to the stage may make the audience members more than a little worried about the speaker's ability.

Once you have taken your place on the stage, it is important to build upon what the introduction did for you and to try to connect with the audience. Just launching into your speech and talking over the heads of the audience will do nothing to establish this all-important connection. On the subject of connecting with an audience, professional speaker, Izzy Gesell suggests the following:

1) Share some information that shows that you know something about the audience or that you appreciate something about them. For example:

> *It's been six years already since I last visited your fine city. I always promised myself that I'd be back, and judging from the warm reception I have received since my arrival, I know I made the right decision to come back.*

2) Show that your interests or concerns and those of the audience coincide.

3) Ask a question that requires a response of sorts, such as having audience members raise their hands. Give careful thought to the question so that it fits naturally with your overall theme. If you want audience members to raise their hands, you may want to give them a cue by raising your own hand just when you expect them to do so. Also, you can prime the audience by alerting them that, shortly, you would be asking a question that requires a response. This helps to keep everybody attentive.

> For example:

> *What is most precious to you? For my ten-year old nephew, there is no question that his Sony PlayStation 3 is pretty precious. And for my 22-year-old niece, there is no question that the big rock on her finger is pretty precious. What is most precious to you? I'd venture to say, that, for practically everybody here, there might be one or two things in your life that you consider precious. (Speaker raises hand) Let's see by a show of hands how many of you would agree with that.*

Also, be prepared for when audiences are unresponsive. If you are going to seek to engage the audience, be prepared with a joke or some other appropriate comment when you do not get the response you want. For example, speaking to an audience of public speaking students, a speaker said, "Let's see by a show of hands how many here have one or two goals that they would like to achieve in the near future." In an audience of over 50 people, not a single hand went up. The speaker said, "Oh, I can see so many invisible hands. Good." The audience laughed.

4) Make a promise (but one that you can keep!). For instance,

> *By the time we finish this seminar, you'll know exactly how to make your clients clamor for more of your products without your even asking!*

Practice:

Prepare an introduction to any of the following topics (or one of your own choosing) and include some elements that help you connect with the audience.

- National Soccer Team
- Global Warming
- Winter Fun
- Traveling
- A Memorable Experience
- Beauty Pageants
- Natural Disasters
- Workaholics

Fun Spot 31: Commonly Confused Words

Research:

	Term	Definition
1	Forbear	
2	Forebear	
3	Gamble	
4	Gambol	
5	Human	
6	Humane	

Notes:

_____
_____
_____
_____
_____
_____
_____
_____
_____
_____
_____
_____

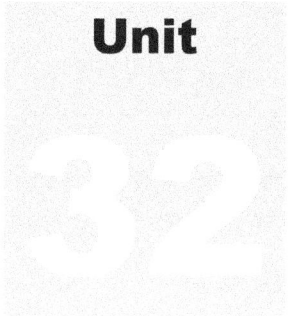

Unit 32

Visual Aids

It has become quite common for presenters to use visual aids such as flip charts, PowerPoint slides or a single chart to highlight some of the points they want to cover.

Visual aids can –

a) add CLARITY to a speech

b) crystallize complex ideas into a few salient points

c) help the audience to focus on the message

d) free the speaker from reading a full text and thus losing connection with the audience

When you are planning to use any form of visual aid, it pays to arrive at the event early to ensure that the proper setup is done. If you can do a dry run, that is, practice your speech using whatever visual aids you have before the audience members start trickling in, all the better.

Ensure that –

a) Your visuals are large enough to be VISIBLE

b) You have only a few lines. Keep it SIMPLE

c) Your writing is LEGIBLE

d) You avoid standing in front of your visual aid

Furthermore,

a) Use color to enhance the images/text (but not too much)

b) Use a thin pointer to direct audience attention to elements on your chart

c) Get audience members involved by inviting some individuals to read what is on the chart

Also,

a) Show a particular visual chart before you begin to talk about it; allow the audience a bit of time to read and absorb the message

b) Remember to talk with the audience, not the chart

c) Ensure that visuals are in the correct order

d) Practice with the visuals ahead of time to ensure that you have the timing right

e) Check spelling or have someone check for you

Practice:

Prepare a speech that allows you to use a visual aid. Use one of the following topics (or one of your own choosing)

a) The Secrets of my success

b) Living a balanced life

c) What Art means to me

d) My country's educational system

e) Fun places I have visited

f) A place that will always have meaning for me

g) Lessons I have learned well

h) What genius means to me

i) The person I used to be

j) The person I hope to be

Fun Spot 32: A Word to the Wise

A speech is poetry:

cadence, rhythm, imagery, sweep!

A speech reminds us that words,

like children,

have the power

to make dance

the dullest beanbag of a heart.

~Peggy Noonan

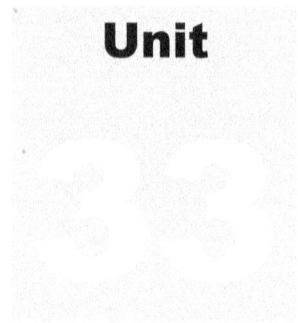

Speech Evaluation: The IMGEPaC Technique

The challenge for a speech evaluator who has to deliver his or her evaluation in front of a large audience shortly after listening to a speech is how to organize the jumble of information and impressions gathered. You have a number of strengths you want to highlight and areas of improvement that you want to mention. By now, you are thoroughly familiar with the use of the Sandwich Technique for evaluation and the CR technique. If you always do your evaluations using one of these two methods, you will be able to get your point across well. You may find, however, that as a speaker, you may be getting stale for using the same pattern all the time.

IMGEPaC is another method that can allow you to deliver a full-fledged evaluation without using any notes. This is because embedded in IMGEPaC is the organizing framework for your evaluation. All you have to do is pay attention to each of the elements.

So what is the IMGEPaC Technique? Simply this:

1) Evaluator starts with an opening statement

2) Evaluator comments on the speaker's

    I   - Introduction

    M   - Message

    G   - Gestures

    E   - Eye contact

    Pa - Pausing / Pacing

    C   - Conclusion (of the Speaker)

3) Evaluator ends with a concluding statement or summary

As a speaker with growing experience, you know how to come up with introductions to a speech. When you are evaluating another speaker, you can also begin with a few general comments about the subject matter and its topicality or relevance to the audience or your impressions of the extent to which the speaker achieved his or her goals. After your preliminary comments, which should take no more than 30 to 45 seconds, you can begin to provide details about the content and delivery of the speech. As always, you are looking for strengths and areas that could be improved. But in what order are you going to present your observations? IMGEPaC allows you to focus on a few key elements and to confine your message to those. Because these are important elements of any speech, feedback in these areas could be helpful to the speaker and also allow you to present your feedback in a compact, easily-digestible format. As with any other speech, you can begin your evaluation with a few personal introductory comments. The elements of IMGEPaC, however, relate to the speaker's content and delivery.

Evaluating with IMGEPaC

Evaluator's Opening Statement	Start with some general comments about the presentation: Was the topic fascinating? Did the speaker make a great impression? Were audience members riveted on the speaker? These are the kinds of comments you do not need to write down but prepare in your mind and allow to flow naturally, signaling to the audience that you are an experienced speaker/evaluator in your own right. If you fumble around with papers and notes trying to read something to the audience, you would lose some of the listeners' attention at this starting gate!
I – INTRODUCTION	How arresting was the speaker's introduction? How did the speaker achieve that effect? Give an example or two.
M – MESSAGE	What was the central message the speaker was trying to convey? Was this clear? Was it confusing? Can you repeat the message?
G – GESTURES	Did the speaker's gestures support the message? Can you give examples of powerful or pertinent gestures used by the speaker?
E – EYE CONTACT	Did the speaker make eye contact? Did the speaker focus too much on one side of the room? Did the speaker focus on only one person, perhaps a key member of the audience to the exclusion of everyone else?
Pa – PAUSING / PACING	Did the speaker speak too fast without breaks? Were the speaker's pauses too long? Did the speaker have a good sense of how to pause for effect?
C – CONCLUSION	Was the speaker's conclusion appropriate? Do you think the conclusion achieved the desired effect? Could the conclusion have been better?
Evaluator's Concluding Statement	The evaluator's concluding statements can be a summary of the strengths of the speaker. Mention how overcoming the area of improvement can help the speaker reach new heights. Be positive, be encouraging, be considerate, be helpful, be empathetic, and be seated.

Evaluating with IMGEPaC - Template

Evaluator's Opening Statement	
I – INTRODUCTION	
M – MESSAGE	
G – GESTURES	
E – EYE CONTACT	
Pa – PAUSING / PACING	
C – CONCLUSION	
Evaluator's Concluding Statement	

Fun Spot 33: Commonly Confused Words

Research:

	Term	Definition
1	Idle	
2	Idol	
3	Incredible	
4	Incredulous	
5	Ingenious	
6	Ingenuous	

Notes:

_____
_____
_____
_____
_____
_____
_____
_____
_____
_____
_____
_____

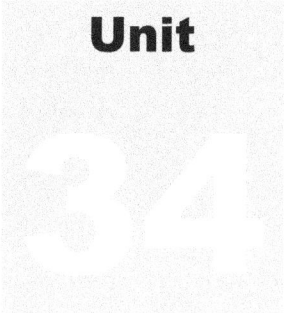

Unit 34

The Power of Persuasion

Human beings are not always so eager to change. Once people are used to a certain idea or way of life, even if it is not exactly superb, they might simply stick to it, month after month, year after year, decade after decade.

From time to time, a person of vision, a person of insight, might take a look at the status quo, that is, the current situation, and realize that it is not acceptable. How to get people to effect change in their own lives or in their environment, however, is a perennial challenge. This is why speakers with persuasive powers are so highly prized.

Your goal as a persuasive speaker may be much more modest than having to persuade a whole nation to abandon age-old practices of a diabolical nature. You may have the task of persuading skeptical colleagues to invest in a new market or to target a new group of clients.

Indeed, persuasion may be as simple as getting others to get excited about something for which they may already have positive feelings (Hawaii anyone?)

Changing people's minds may require you to use a combination of facts and emotion. Nobel Prize winner Al Gore tried to get the world and the U.S. government to take the matter of global warming seriously. In statements regarding global warming Gore made both logical (fact-based) and emotional appeals.

Which is which?

> *The scientists tell us that the tundra in danger of thawing contains an amount of additional global warming pollution that is equal to the total amount that is already in the earth's atmosphere. Similarly, earlier this year, yet another team of scientists reported that the previous twelve months saw 32 glacial earthquakes on Greenland between 4.6 and 5.1 on the Richter scale - a disturbing sign that a massive destabilization may now be underway deep within the second largest accumulation of ice on the planet, enough ice to raise sea level 20 feet (6 m) worldwide if it broke up and slipped into the sea.*

(From speech by Al Gore at New York University School of Law, Monday, 18 September 2006 – Global Warming is an Immediate Crisis)

> *A day will come when our children and grandchildren will look back and they'll ask one of two questions: They will ask, 'What in God's name were they doing?' or they may look back and say, 'How did they find the uncommon moral courage to rise above politics and redeem the promise of American democracy?'*

(Al Gore's Statement to the U.S. Congress on Global Warming, March 21, 2007)

> *The absence of the United States from the treaty means that 25% of the world economy is now missing. It is like filling a bucket with a large hole in the bottom. When the United States eventually joins the rest of the world community in making this system operate well, the global market for carbon emissions will become a highly efficient closed system and every corporate board of directors on earth will have a fiduciary duty to manage and reduce CO_2 emissions in order to protect shareholder value.*

(From speech by Al Gore at New York University School of Law, Monday, 18 September, 2006 – Global Warming is an Immediate Crisis)

Some persuasive speeches are direct about seeking action from the audience. In the case of Gore, he wanted to persuade nations and individuals to do what it takes to save the earth. Your goal as a persuasive speaker may simply be to persuade listeners to make a contribution to a charity that you believe in or for potential clients to purchase your product.

Appealing to Self-interest

Appealing to a person's self-interest is also one of the best ways to persuade people. In other words, people are interested in the question of "What's in it for them?" Why should they do what they are being asked to do? How would they benefit if they donated money to a group of people suffering half way around the world? That is more than a fair question.

The contribution of the United States to the developing world had been criticized for many years as being paltry. It did not help that the Bush (Number 43) administration rejected many calls to contribute more money towards the fight for AIDS in Africa. How did the US begin to change its stance on the issue? When Colin Powell, former Secretary of State in the Bush administration pointed out that AIDS in Africa was a security issue for the United States. George W. Bush, the 43rd president of the United States, and other administration leaders woke up. In other words, by crafting the issue not in terms of the benefits to the suffering AIDS patients but in terms of how important it is for Americans to be safe from harm, the US government began to take action.

Here is the connection Powell made: AIDS often leads to the death of millions of people, leading to state failure. When there are no able-bodied people in a country to work, the economy cannot function. When there is such a failure, this creates a vacuum for terrorists to come in and take control. Such terrorists, of course, could then threaten the interests of America, because they have a safe place to operate from and can also recruit other potential terrorists from among the people whose lives are being ravaged by disease. In short, helping people in Africa who have AIDS is not just a matter of charity; it is one way by which America can save itself from future terrorists!

Here is a summary of factors to take into consideration when attempting to persuade others.

- Offer evidence to support your appeals.

- Highlight your qualification for discussing the particular issue. Is it based on academic background, or a close personal experience of the issue?

- Let the audience feel your passion. A lifeless delivery will have little or no effect.

- Avoid being memorable for being boring.

- You must appear not only confident and knowledgeable but also caring. Your demeanor is important.

- You might want to highlight some of the arguments often raised against your position and proceed to show why those criticisms are not valid. In doing this, do not condemn those who do not agree with you. You may indeed have some of those critics in your audience!

- Wrap your logic in a shroud of emotion and you cannot fail to persuade. Logic and emotion together as one – that is the proverbial ticket.

Fun Spot 34: A Word to the Wise

But I... never could make a good impromptu speech without several hours to prepare it.

~Mark Twain, 1879 speech *(Thanks, Garson O'Toole!)*

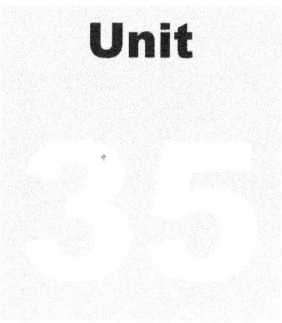

Can You Inspire? Moving to Higher Ground

There are times when people with great potential simply do not recognize their hidden talents. Other times, people are aware that they have some gifts but they are not motivated to do anything much about these abilities. An inspirational speech rouses people out of their stupor and makes them see new possibilities that they may either have ignored or not been aware of.

Your audience may be personally, emotionally, professionally, or financially stagnant and just need the right words to pick them up and get them motivated to do something about the situation.

To be a good inspirational speaker, you obviously need to understand people's feelings, desires, hopes, and fears and to articulate how it is that tomorrow could be a better day. For those who have lost hope, you may have to sketch why the current moment is fertile for effecting change. After all, some might have tried before and failed. Why should they try again?

Inspiring people does not mean coddling them. It often means challenging them to reach into themselves for resources that are hidden in order to make visible change — in themselves or in their environment. When John F. Kennedy said, "Ask not what your country can do for you; ask what you can do for your country," he unleashed a generation of people who felt that they could change the world and change the image of America for the better. And when in 2008, Barack Obama said that the problem was not the American people and that the American people were part of the solution, he tapped into a deep well of pride and longing for change among the American people, along with the feeling that the American people could join together to effect a big change.

To be inspirational:

- Establish a connection with the audience, a deep connection if possible.
- Show that you understand the current environment and that while things might be difficult there are also indications that the time is ripe for change. (If not now, when?)
- Highlight the qualities that the audience members possess that give you the confidence that they can change the status quo.
- Avoid glossing over difficulties; instead, show how and why it should be possible to surmount those difficulties.
- Use quotations, stories, etc. to reach both the mind and the heart.

As Obama emphasized repeatedly during his 2008 campaign, "We are the change we have been waiting for."

Why not use your own gifts of eloquence to empower, motivate, and lead?

Fun Spot 35: Commonly Confused Words

Research:

	Term	Definition
1	Irrelevant	
2	Irreverent	
3	Lightening	
4	Lightning	
5	Miner	
6	Minor	

Notes:

_____
_____
_____
_____
_____
_____
_____
_____
_____
_____
_____
_____

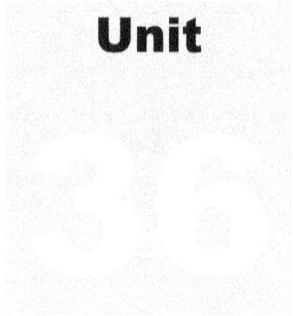

Handling Questions and Answers

Some public speakers are uncomfortable with having to answer questions in midstream, that is, while they are in the middle of a presentation. They would rather complete their presentation and then handle questions. If that is the case with you, it might be a good idea to inform the audience at the beginning of the presentation so that you can deliver your piece in peace. Likewise, if you are comfortable taking questions during the course of your presentation, you might want to mention it. It is difficult for audience members to determine which of these two categories of speakers you fall into until you have informed them, right?

Questions from the audience should be seen as an opportunity rather than a crisis-inducing moment. A careful speaker can anticipate what questions might arise (I'm glad you asked that question!).

There are times when a question is not as clear as could be. Check with the questioner to ensure that you understand. You may do this by rephrasing the question and asking the questioner if your interpretation is correct.

If you absolutely do not know the answer, admit it. It is far better to say that you will look for the answer than to speculate and answer incorrectly, with some possible damage to your credibility; thankfully, nobody knows everything so such an admission is not as dreadful as it might seem. If you are so ill-prepared that you cannot handle any and all questions, then that might indeed look bad. If you have taken time to prepare your speech and to dig into the background of your topic, such a problem, however, is unlikely to occur.

Be tactful and avoid losing your cool or putting people down. Those are not ways to endear oneself to an audience. There are times when you might have to deflect questions because they are too sensitive or personal. Be frank if you feel you cannot answer some kinds of questions. Also, some questions might be unrelated to the topic at hand and might be a distraction. Those also you might have to deflect tactfully.

Some people are fond of asking long questions with multiple parts. You might want to remind your audience members to keep their questions short or try to get to the point quickly. Some people also prefer to make their own long speech before asking a question. Tactfully, remind them that you are waiting for the question. When you get a long, multi-pronged question, it is easy to fumble when you remember only one part of the question. In such a case, you might want to break up the question and answer them one at a time. You might jot down each of the questions on a pad, using key words to jog your memory.

There is no better way to impress an audience, however, than to get a multi-pronged question and to deftly answer them one at a time. You come across as a truly intelligent soul and you have an opportunity to cement your reputation as an expert of sorts. Good luck.

Scatterbrained

One famous American entertainer spoke once at an achievement academy for high school students. The entertainer, though having given a great speech, was almost completely at sea during the question and answer period.

Some of the questions from the students had two or three parts. At times, the speaker would answer the second part and forget the first. Sometimes, he answered the first and forgot about the second one. Audience members had to keep reminding him about the questions. There was no question that people loved him and respected him…for his music. He did not make a good impression in the question and answer period.

How could this entertainer have avoided the kind of problems he faced?

An Orderly Mind

In another case, after the speaker had talked about the law for an hour, he introduced the question and answer session. Here was the plan. People could ask questions, one by one. He wrote down all the questions, about ten of them. He studied the questions for a few seconds and announced that there were some common themes. Then he divided the questions into three broad themes.

He used the questions as memory joggers, and created a point-form outline from which he gave another shorter speech in which he answered all the questions posed. It was delightful to listen to the speech. There was no sense of confusion. The audience seemed quite satisfied.

Fun Spot 36: A Word to the Wise

Make sure you have finished speaking before your audience has finished listening.

~ Dorothy Sarnoff

Unit 37

Making Numbers Make Sense

If you say that there are ten rooms in a house, practically anyone can picture it. Of course, listeners' experiences would come into play in terms of how they would imagine this ten-room house. The image that a Hollywood heiress will have of a ten-room house may be vastly different from that of a young boy who has lived in a shack all his life – hopefully, this child can also count to ten!

Big numbers and unfamiliar units present difficulty for many people. For example, if you heard the following, are you able to picture it?

> *The country covers an area of 776,788,999 square meters!*

Do you have any clue how big this is?

> *The Amazon is being depleted at a rate of 659,000 hectares a day.*

Does that help you? Can you make sense of these numbers?

To make numbers make better sense it is often necessary to relate them to other more familiar elements. For example, any Japanese has an idea of the standard size of a traditional mat, a *tatami*, making it easy for Japanese to picture the size of a 6-tatami room.

A person who has just entered Japan may not have any idea what size mat is being used as the measure and might have to be instructed with arm spans or comparison with something concrete that the listener can relate to, see, or imagine.

For the uninitiated, according to Wikipedia, the popular online encyclopedia, in Japan,

> *The traditional dimensions of the mats were fixed at 90 cm by 180 cm (1.62 square meters) by 5 cm (35.5 in by 71 in by 2 in). Half-mats, 90 cm by 90 cm (35.5 in by 35.5 in) are also made. Shops were traditionally designed to be 5 ½ mats (8.91 m2),*

and tearooms and teahouses are frequently 4 ½ mats (7.29 m^2).
(Tatami http://www.en.wikipedia.org/wiki/Tatami)

Just throwing numbers at a reader or audience members can be, shall we say, unexciting; put some thought into breaking the numbers down in ways that the average person, even a child can understand. Let's see how some writers explain nanotechnology to those of us who may not be familiar with this increasingly important field.

One nanometer is 10^{-9} m. By comparison, a human hair is approximately 70,000 nm in diameter, a red blood cell is approximately 5,000 nm wide and simple organic molecules have sizes ranging from 0.5 to 5 nm.
(http://www.iom-world.org/research/nanoparticles.php)

In the above, the numbers themselves do not have a big impact. The comparison with human hair, however, brings the subject alive.

On the same topic, Carole Bass writes:

Nanotechnology involves the manipulation of teeny particles, measuring between one and 100 nanometers. (A nanometer is one billionth of a meter, or roughly 80,000 times smaller than the width of a human hair.)....Physically, nanoparticles are so minute that they can penetrate deep into the body. (Bass p.1)

Are you sufficiently concerned now?

Here's how another writer discusses homelessness in Japan, making a comparison that brings the matter into better perspective.

In Tokyo alone, the number of homeless has swelled to 5,700, more than double that of five years ago. The world's second-largest economy now has at least 20,500 homeless. This may pale in comparison with the U.S., a country with twice Japan's population and about 750,000 homeless "on any given night," according to the National Alliance to End Homelessness in Washington…(Prusher 2001 pg1).

To make numbers make sense, you need to take time to think carefully about your audience and how you can convert the raw numbers at hand to something that will be both clear and meaningful for them. It may seem irksome to have to take extra time to think of the best mental image to bring your numbers to life. When you make your speech and you present your numbers and you see the light of understanding in the eyes of your listeners, you will realize that the extra effort was well worth it.

Fun Spot 37: Commonly Confused Words

Research:

	Term	Definition
1	Moral	
2	Morale	
3	Plain	
4	Plane	
5	Practical	
6	Practicable	

Notes:

_____
_____
_____
_____
_____
_____
_____
_____
_____
_____
_____
_____

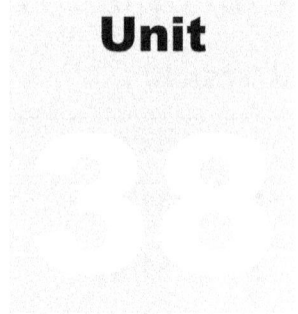

Speaking With an Eye on the Clock

When a television program is scheduled to run for thirty minutes, that is pretty much what you get. And when you've paid for a 60-second advertising spot during the Super Bowl, you can't plead for an extra 7 seconds because that is how long your advertisement is. Fair is fair.

Time, clearly, is important, but in some settings there is a greater demand for speakers' having to adhere to time.

If you are scheduled to speak for an hour and you speak for an extra two minutes you might be forgiven by the audience especially if you have the audience members at the edge of their seats. And if you are scheduled to speak for fifteen minutes and you go on for another minute or so, the audience might be able to live with it.

But imagine being scheduled to speak for ten minutes and choosing to speak for thirty! You would be glad to get out alive!

Speakers who are able to adhere to time requirements make a better impression and are probably more likely to be invited back.

One obvious way to ensure that you speak within the allotted time is to practice using a timer. If you find your initial effort too long, carefully go through the materials. You may find some points that can be deleted without much loss to your overall theme and presentation.

You may also want to keep a timer or watch close by while speaking, perhaps on the lectern. If you are speaking without the benefit of a lectern, you do not want to be seen checking your wristwatch every few minutes. At the famous TED Conference (www.ted.com), the speaker has the benefit of a big clock on the stage that tells exactly how much time is left. You may have to rely on someone giving you some signals regarding the time or when you have spoken for a considerable amount of time, you can openly ask the MC: "How much time do I have left?" If you are using a lectern, of course, you can discreetly take a peek at the timepiece you've placed on it to learn how much time you have left. You could then adjust the rest of your speech by cutting something unimportant out if the speech is too long. Conversely, if you realize that you have much more time than you had envisioned, you might consider adding another point or two, to ensure that you finish within the expected time allotment. If you are fortunate enough to have a huge clock staring at you from the back of the room, you are all the better for it. Happy speaking – with an eye forever on the clock.

Fun Spot 38: A Word to the Wise

The most important question to ask on the job is not "What am I getting?" The most important question to ask on the job is "What am I becoming?"

- Jim Rohn (Motivational Speaker)

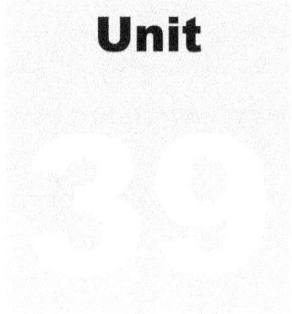

Extemporaneous Speaking – The Pleasure and the Peril

Being able to speak extemporaneously is a highly valued skill. You attend a friend's party. It turns out to be a really big party, and the people at the party are not just interested in playing games but want some intellectual stimulation as well. Knowing that you have traveled the world, the host claps her hands and gets everybody's attention. "Aren't we lucky?" she announces, clearing her throat. "Aren't we lucky…Aren't we lucky that we have with us here today Ms. Gina Perez? My good friend Gina has traveled around the world two or three times over. She must be able to share some insights with those of us who feel stuck at home all the time. Gina, why don't you speak for a few minutes about what it takes to be an intrepid world traveler?"

Everybody starts clapping. And there you are. You have indeed traveled the world. And you do indeed have a lot of stories to tell. But tonight, you don't even know where to begin.

Some of the individuals who have made a name for themselves as great speakers – Mark Twain and Winston Churchill come to mind – took a lot of time to prepare speeches that seemed like impromptu speeches. In other words, if you know that there is any chance you might be called to speak, prepare a rough outline in your mind. For example, you might think, "If I am called upon to speak about my travels, I will talk about my original fear of travel and my first experience of traveling to Bali. I will then talk about the hike I took with my two buddies to the Himalayas and round it off with the week I spent with Aborigines in Australia."

Such a mental outline may be all you need to regale the audience because you have a rough structure in place and you are talking about something that comes out of your own deep experience.

You have access to all the information you need. What you need is just a bit of organization: What you should talk about first, second, and third, and that is all there is to it. You will not be asked to speak extemporaneously about something for which you have no expertise. Someone might ask you to speak without preparation only because the person knows you have a close and intimate connection to a particular experience or field of endeavor and that such knowledge is sufficient to make you a passably good speaker on the subject. The short-notice speech template, along with Quick Intro and other techniques covered such as PREP and PPF can all come to your rescue when called upon to give an extemporaneous speech. Are you ready?

For each of the following topics, think of three points you want to cover. Add an introduction. Decide on a conclusion. Stir it up with some examples and stories and you are ready to give your extemporaneous speech.

Speaking exercise

Prepare a 5-7 minute speech on any of the following topics:

(Plus or minus 30 seconds is acceptable)

1) The generation gap
2) Mistakes I have made
3) A day to remember
4) My hero
5) Samurai spirit
6) Mountain climbing
7) My advice to the next generation
8) What gives me peace of mind
9) My favorite period in history

Fun Spot 39: Commonly Confused Words

Research:

	Term	Definition
1	Pray	
2	Prey	
3	Principal	
4	Principle	
5	Raise	
6	Raze	

Notes:

_____
_____
_____
_____
_____
_____
_____
_____
_____
_____
_____
_____

Fun Spot 39: Commonly Confused Words

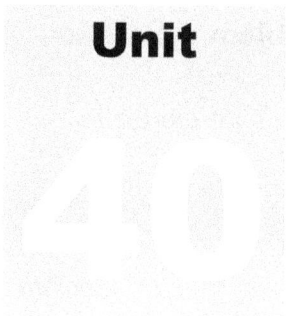

Unit 40

Impromptu Speaking: Advanced Techniques 1

In your daily experience of life, whether in business or otherwise, you may be called upon from time to time to offer advice, share opinions, or make comments on one issue or the other. In most cases, you simply draw upon your professional and personal experience to respond calmly to the request. In public speaking forums, however because of pressure, it is possible to experience false starts, muddled thoughts, or even go blank. You can make things easier for yourself if you internalize a number of frameworks such as the ones below. These are not necessarily easy to use at the beginning but once you master them they can help guide your thoughts and make you sound like a truly polished speaker.

a) Problem + Solution

Some topics can be tackled in the form of a problem and a solution. Naturally, some issues are much more easily cast in this mode than others. For example, the topic of <u>pollution</u> is a problem and does not take much imagination to think about it in that way. What about food? Normally, food is a necessity, a good thing but there are ways in which you can talk about food as a problem...along with a related solution.

If you want to have fun and sharpen your thinking and speaking skills, try using Problem + Solution on subjects and topics that are not usually viewed as problems.

It is a challenging exercise to try to talk about such generally positive topics as Ice Cream, Sleep, Fresh Air, Sunshine, as though they were problems. But comedians often pull it off. For example, most people are apt to think of children as adorable, and yet, comedians are often able to paint a picture of children that is contrary to this view, which may nevertheless leave you laughing. Comedians often look at everyday issues from different angles. To be a successful public speaker you also need to cultivate the habit of examining issues from different perspectives.

Model Impromptu Speech
Problem + Solution: Addicted to Chocolate

Here's an example.

> *My topic is food. Like most people I love food, especially chocolate, and that is a problem. It's a problem because I do not eat chocolate only once in a while. I eat chocolate everyday. In the morning, I have two bars of chocolate, and in the afternoon, I have another two. And just before I go to bed, I eat a bar or two of my favorite, called Dars.*
>
> *Obviously, the taste of chocolate is not a problem for me but recently with all the talk about so-called metabolic syndrome, namely bloated belly syndrome, I am beginning to get worried. Looking at me it may not seem that I should have much reason to worry but I have gained a few pounds in the last few months and I am sure that I am going to gain even more over time. How do I know that I am going to gain more weight?*
>
> *It's simple. I do not have any intention of giving up chocolate. I love chocolate and I cannot lie about it. I have tried to reduce my consumption from time to time but I always end up eating more and more.*
>
> *Anyway, the only way to prevent me from eating chocolate is to ban all the chocolate companies from selling this well-loved delicacy, and as we know, this is unlikely to happen any time soon. I have also enlisted my friends to help me stop but some of them love chocolate even more than I do so that has not helped. For now, I am not in any imminent danger but I will continue to try to reduce my chocolate intake. Chocolate is a problem but an even greater problem is my attempt to stop indulging in it: if you have a workable solution, please let me know.*

b) PRS: Problem, Reaction, Solution

P: A baby is hungry.

R: The baby cries.

S: A parent feeds the baby.

Usually, when there is a problem, such as a mix-up, an earthquake, a lost item of considerable importance, the people connected to the issue might react differently from one another. While some might take their loss with a shrug of the shoulder (it can't be helped), others might wail and moan and talk through their grief. Still others might take off from the scene of the unpleasant encounter and stay away for a long time, until perhaps the memories of pain have become sufficiently dim.

The wide variety of responses that people express in the face of a conundrum, a problem, a difficulty, can offer rich opportunities for storytelling and provide color to a table topic (impromptu speaking). This applies as well for public speaking practice purposes as for real situations.

If the story has a happy ending or an unexpected outcome, all the better. So, when confronted with a topic that focuses on a problem, you can talk a little bit about the problem, talk about the reaction of some of the people caught within the problem, and then finish with what solution, if any, was found to the problem.

c) PCS: Problem, Cause, Solution

PCS is not unlike PRS. You begin with the problem. What is it? What are the symptoms? Whom does it affect? Is it a big problem or a small problem? Why should the audience be concerned about it?

After elaborating on the problem enough to get audience members sufficiently interested (or worried, as the case may be), you outline the causes of the problem. If you do not know the cause, you can talk about what some experts or some people concerned about the issue think is the cause.

Finally, you outline a possible solution to the problem.

Practice: Use PRS or PCS to talk about the following

1) Shark attacks on swimmers
2) Neglectful parents
3) Debris in space
4) Falling educational standards
5) Leadership vacuum
6) Illegal Sale of Ivory
7) Nuclear Power Accidents
8) Food poisoning
9) Beaches
10) Vacation
11) Sweets
12) Close friendships
13) Perfectionism
14) Blind dates
15) Shopping online

Fun Spot 40: A Word to the Wise

Our attitudes control our lives.

Attitudes are a secret power working 24 hours a day, for good or bad. It is of paramount importance that we know how to harness and control this great force.

~ Tom Blandi

Unit 41

Impromptu Speaking: Advanced Techniques 2

a) Bait and Switch: A Desperate Maneuver

According to the Merriam Webster dictionary, bait and switch is "a sales tactic in which a customer is attracted by the advertisement of a low-priced item but is then encouraged to buy a higher-priced one" or "the ploy of offering a person something desirable to gain favor (as political support) then thwarting expectations with something less desirable."

It is clear that this method does not have positive associations and is probably only best used as a last resort. With this in mind you may have heard the apocryphal story of the biology student who studied the subject of birds all semester and was shocked to see that his exam had only one question: Trees.

Here is how this student handled it, giving you a clue to how you might also handle a particularly difficult table topic.

> *Trees are living things. They can be found lining the sides of streets in major cities. But they are found in even greater numbers outside the city. Indeed, a tight collection of trees in a large area might very well be what we call a forest. Trees are popular places for birds to build their nests. Now, one may ask, "What is a bird?" ...*

The student then wrote ten pages about birds, with detailed diagrams. Needless to say, he got an A+!

Likewise, in table topics, you can maneuver the topic so that it is one that you can talk about comfortably. Only be sure to refer to the original topic in your conclusion. With any luck, the audience may have forgotten what you were supposed to speak on initially. Obviously, this is a technique that you would want to use only if you feel that you have been backed into a corner.

Let's say, your topic is Totoro but you know very little about this animation character. You are much more comfortable with Doraemon because you have read Doraemon manga and watched some Doraemon-related animation.

Here's one possible way to do your bait and switch.

> *My topic is Totoro, who, I believe is a popular animation character in Japan and around the world. Stories like that of Totoro are very precious because they connect us with magic and wonder...much like my favorite character, Doraemon, a cat that has come to the present from the future. Doraemon is endearing to me and many other people because he has a range of tools that make it possible to solve practically any problem that he or his friend, Nobito, encounter. This makes me wonder how wonderful and magical life would be for me and many others if we had similar tools to wipe away our troubles and bring back the joy of life when things go wrong. You may have heard of Doraemon's so-called ankipan, a piece of bread that aids memory when eaten. I wish I had eaten some ankipan this morning so I could remember what little I know of animation characters. In any case, whether we are talking about Totoro, Doraemon, or Hello Kitty, the main thing to remember is that these characters can help ease the boredom of our lives. They can transport us into another world where everything is possible. So, let's make a toast to Totoro, Doraemon, and all the animation characters that touch our hearts and help make life a little more bearable, a little more fun, from day to day!*

Remember, for table topics practice, you are only supposed to speak for 1½ to 2 minutes so by the time you've taken a little detour and decided to return to the original topic, your time may already be up. Congratulations!!!

You may bow now.

b) What Would So-and-so Say about Such-and-such?

So-and-so could be anyone that you know a great deal about. For some people, So-and-so could be Jesus, Gandhi, Samurai, Communists, Feminists, the President of your country, Capitalists, Greenpeace, Economists, your Grandmother, or Confucius!

Each of the above, and many other familiar figures or groups, are known for having certain strong views, values, or outlooks on life, and so you can address various topics by considering what these individuals, groups, or characters might have said or would say.

Let's say your topic is "Respect."

What would a Feminist say about Respect?

My topic is respect and when I consider this topic I cannot help but consider what feminists think about this word. Throughout history, women have felt the sting of oppression. Women have worked hard without their efforts being respected. Women have toiled in the fields and in their homes, cooking and cleaning and taking care of their husbands and children but they never got any respect for their efforts.

Even in those countries that pride themselves on being democratic, just a few decades ago, women could not vote. And so, even today, women continue to fight for an equal playing field and to seek recognition and respect for their achievements. To some extent, women have been able to fight for the chance to be educated, at least in countries such as Japan, the United States and in recent years, Singapore. It is also encouraging to learn that in North America, there are more women than men in college, but do women get the respect they need and deserve? No, no, no.

In many countries women are still paid less than men even though they may do more work than their male counterparts. In fairness, there are a few countries where women are beginning to get true respect. The Scandinavian countries are in the lead. In Sweden and Denmark women can be found in many positions of leadership and these women have been able to champion laws that show that they understand the needs of women. In Japan, women still have a long way to go but as women continue to study and fight for their rights, there are indications that such respect will come, hopefully, soon, rather than later.

What would a Communist say about Respect?

Workers need respect and they need it now! Throughout history, capitalists have exploited the labor of working people, sucking the blood out of the worker until he is no longer of any use. That has been the history of working people, toiling while those who control capital continue to enjoy the fruits of such labor.

You can understand why in the former Soviet Union and in many other countries workers stood up to fight for their rights. Here in this country, is there any exploitation? We might say that conditions have improved greatly but many workers are still afraid to stand up for their rights. They fear that they will lose their livelihood if they make too much noise.

Communists, or even their milder cousins, socialists, will certainly not stand for a situation where workers have no rights. Now, I am not saying that we should change our nation into a communist state. It is obvious that communism did not work in the former Soviet Union, and many other places but there is also no question that some communist ideas make a great deal of sense, at least in theory. What is wrong with showing some respect to the ordinary men and women who break their backs everyday to make sure that the country is well supplied with products that we need? Everybody needs respect, the worker as well as the boss, wouldn't you agree?

Practice:

1) What would a samurai warrior say about respect? Think about it.
2) What would Mother Teresa say about war?
3) What would an astronaut say about canceling the space program?
4) What would your grandmother say about giving mobile phones to children?

What would _____ say about _____?

What would _____ say about _____?

What would _____ say about _____?

Fun Spot 41: Commonly Confused Words

Research:

	Term	Definition
1	Sensible	
2	Sensitive	
3	Stationary	
4	Stationery	
5	Straight	
6	Strait	

Notes:

_____
_____
_____
_____
_____
_____
_____
_____
_____
_____
_____
_____

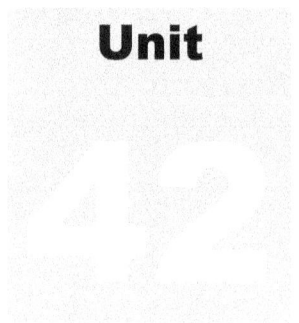

Impromptu Speaking: Advanced Techniques 3

The following techniques may be familiar to business students as frameworks for analysis. There is no reason why they should be confined only to the boardroom. These frameworks can allow you to talk intelligently about a vast number of topics, whether in the barroom, the ballroom, or the boardroom.

a) PESTLE

Students of commerce are likely to be familiar with –

PESTLE

Political

Economic

Social

Technological

Legal

Environmental

This framework can guide your discussion of a table topic or speech. There are any number of topics that can be considered from such a multi-pronged approach.

Let's say your topic is Computers.

P – Political: *Computers have become very much a part of our everyday existence and many of us take them for granted. From a political point of view, some governments have come to realize that their citizens will remain behind unless given the opportunity to join the computer age. Knowledge is power, remember? This is why some governments such as those of Brazil, Nigeria,* *and Egypt have signed on to the so-called One Laptop per Child program. Through this program, children in developing countries can obtain laptops for only one hundred dollars or so, paid for by their governments. This will empower the children to step into the future with confidence.*

E – Economic: *Also, computers can make an economic difference. In Borneo, some farmers are advertising their products online and are able to make sales of their products to people from all over the world. Even though they are far from the major centers of commerce and capital, technology is able to put them in touch with people who are willing to pay for their products. This has made a big difference in their economic situation. And it's not only in Borneo; many people around the world are able to sell their products directly, whether on eBay or Yahoo auctions so that they can make that extra bit of money that can make all the difference in their economic situation.*

S – Social: *For the social, need I say that for those who are shut in because they are sick, computers, the Internet, can become a real lifeline. In Hong Kong, for example, a young man who had become paralyzed following a freak accident posted a message online that he was tired of living and was going to commit suicide. He received thousands of messages asking him to give life a chance. He decided to live and has found joy in the thousands of friends who communicate with him daily. So computers can give a boost to one's social life and help build community that stretches beyond one's neighborhood, town, or even country.*

T – Technological: *As a technological device, the computer may be in its infancy and yet consider all the things it allows us to do. It is useful to an accountant who wants to do some calculations on a spreadsheet and to the young child who just wants to draw or doodle. And let me say that the technology may be no less important to the musician who uses the computer to create or store music. It would be interesting to see how computer technology develops further but there is no question that the best is yet to come.*

L – Legal: *Since computers became connected with one another in the form of the Internet, legal issues have arisen almost without stop. There was the issue of illegal downloading of music and sharing of music files which have led to numerous lawsuits from the music industry. And then there is the issue of hacking. Companies like Sony have had their websites hacked, sometimes leading to the exposure of private details of clients. Some hackers have been arrested and prosecuted while many others lurk within the shadows of cyberspace, ready to strike. International legal cooperation will be essential if this problem is to be brought under any measure of control.*

E – Environmental   *As much as many of us have come to love our computers and the Internet, we cannot escape the reality that computers contribute to environmental degradation. People are buying new computers every three or four years. What happens to the old computers? Some of these are recycled but there are also toxic materials in computers that can pose a health hazard to the poor people who end up tearing these old computers apart. Fortunately, many computer manufacturers are trying to be responsible so there are arrangements that allow retail shops to collect old computers so that they do not simply end up in the landfill and become an environmental hazard that haunts humanity for ages.*

b) SWOT

This is another business-related acronym that can serve as aid in communicating your thoughts.

SWOT stands for:

- **Strengths**
- **Weaknesses**
- **Opportunities**
- **Threats**

Take a topic such as Talent Shows, Amusement Parks, or your neighborhood Tennis Club. For each of these, what are the strengths, the weaknesses, the opportunities available and the potential threats associated with them?

With all these tools for table topics at your finger tips, table topics is bound to be a whole lot of fun – if you practice, and practice, and practice.

SWOT Grid

Strengths	Weaknesses

Opportunities	Threats

Can you see how SWOT and PESTLE can help you organize your thoughts for delivering a coherent speech?

Topics for Practice
(PESTLE & SWOT)

1) My country's economic prospects

2) Space travel

3) Underwater exploration

4) Starting a new business

5) Arresting desertification

6) Genetically modified crops

7) Electric vehicles

8) Building factories in countries with low labor cost

9) Hosting the Olympics

10) Dealing with sea piracy

Fun Spot 42: A Word to the Wise

There is one quality that one must possess to win, and that is definiteness of purpose, the knowledge of what one wants, and a burning desire to possess it.

~ Napoleon Hill

Unit

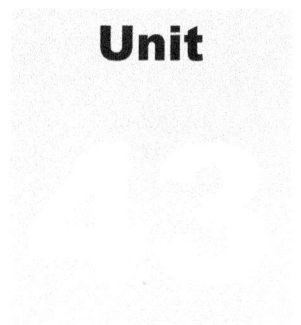

Speech Evaluation: The GLOVE Technique

From award-winning Toastmaster, Matthew Ownby, comes the following template for winning evaluations.

Note: Please write specific examples found in the speech

+	↑	Reminders
<u>Gestures</u>	G	- No distracting repetitive movements - Gestures matched message - Maintained eye contact
<u>Language</u>	L	- Didn't use jargon - Clear/concise - Word choice - Used rhetorical techniques
<u>Organization</u>	O	- Clear opening, body, and conclusion - Well-defined transitions - No non-sequiturs
<u>Vocal Variety</u>	V	- Wasn't too fast or slow - Varied pitch and timbre when appropriate - Good voice projection
<u>Extra Material</u>	E	- Complements the speech - Didn't distract from the message - Legible for far away audience members
Message:		Clear and obvious
Opening:		Good hooks
Closing:		Good closure/positive tone

Guaranteed Formula for Public Speaking

Fun Spot 43: Commonly Confused Words

Research:

	Term	Definition
1	Suit	
2	Suite	
3	Systematic	
4	Systemic	
5	Wave	
6	Waive	

Notes:

_____
_____
_____
_____
_____
_____
_____
_____
_____
_____
_____
_____

Fun Spot 43: Commonly Confused Words

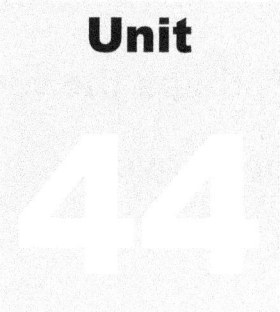

Unit 44

When YOU are the Master of Ceremonies

Congratulations! You have been asked to serve as Master of Ceremonies (MC). What an honor. The day of the event is fast approaching and your excitement is quickly giving way to flutters of nervousness. Take a deep breath. No need to panic. It's time to take action.

First of all, it is important to reflect on the fact that you were asked to be MC because someone believed in you; someone believed in you enough, to give you the opportunity. Or better still, you might have felt a surge of confidence that convinced you to volunteer for the role. Both are good signs and now is not the time to throw away that momentary surge in confidence. Serving as an MC can be yet another opportunity to aim for a new level of achievement. With the proper preparation and commitment to excellence, before you know it, you will be talking about this experience of serving as an MC in the past tense. And it will have become one of your many accomplishments.

Rather than worrying about what might go wrong on the appointed day, why not begin to work towards making it one of the best days of your life?

If you break down your MC role into three parts, you will realize that it is quite a manageable feat. There are things you have to do <u>before the event</u>, things you do <u>during the event</u>, and others you engage in <u>after the event</u>.

Fun Spot 44: A Word to the Wise

Perhaps the very best question that you can memorize and repeat, over and over, is, "what is the most valuable use of my time right now?"

~ Brian Tracy

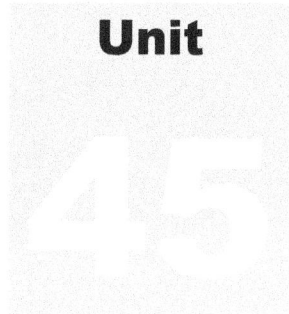

Unit 45

The MC Role: Before the Event

Almost as soon as you know that you are going to serve as MC, keep an open line of communication with those who can assist you to make the event a success. This involves two groups of people: a) those connected with the administrative aspects of the event – organizers, managers, or liaison officers and b) those who will be playing a role on the day of the event – speakers, performers, timers, or judges.

Naturally, some individuals can be found in both camps.

Is there an agenda?

It is possible that the event for which you are going to be the MC is an already established event and that there is a standard format for the program. Find out if sample agendas or program outlines are available. It is possible that even if such programs exist, certain elements of the program could be improved upon. By asking questions about past events you should be able to get an idea of how much you need to retain from the old way of doing things and how much you could add to enhance the program.

Without talking to key stakeholders, you are unlikely to be able to make the proper decisions regarding such matters. Talking to those who have a role on the day of the event will also allow you to understand elements such as time needed and any special props that are necessary.

Here is a simple sample agenda for a workshop for new recruits.

EAST-WEST INC. -- TRAIN THE TRAINER WORKSHOP
Location: Sylph Centre, 1761 Blanshard Street, Singapore

Date: December 7, 2010

8:00 a.m.	Welcome/Coffee & Tea	
8:30	Session opens	Mr. Ping-Ping Tang (MC)
8:35	Company president's remarks	Ms. Erika Yamataka
8:45	Negotiation Mastery Workshop	Ms. Fatima Springsteen
10:45	Break (15 minutes)	
11:00	Karma & Charisma	Mr. Vikas Van der Hoof
1:00 p.m.	Close	
1:05	Photo session	
1:15	Free lunch	

Make the agenda attractive looking, not in a decorative sense, but in terms of layout and the use of white space. If the agenda is too cluttered, it will not be inviting to participants. You want people to find what they want quickly on the agenda, not look at it like a puzzle to be solved. Group similar items and make use of logical breaks to help readers understand the program easily.

Clarify the Purpose

The purpose of the event may be clear enough if you are intimately connected with the group or event for which you are to serve as MC. If you are dealing with an organization or group that you do not know very well, it would be wise to clarify with key individuals what the purpose and expectations are.

Is it

- a speech competition?
- a corporate holiday celebration?

- an end-of-year awards program?
- a roast?

If you have doubts about any aspect of the event, please talk to those who ought to know, so that there are no unfortunate surprises on the day of the event.

Know the Audience

The more you know about who your audience members are going to be, the better you can plan with their needs in mind. The author recalls attending a humorous speech competition once. Some of the participants may not have been aware that children would attend the event. Their adult-oriented, off-color jokes were met with silence. With so many children sprinkled throughout the audience, there was a palpable feeling that this was not a good place to be telling those kinds of jokes. If the contestants in question had asked more questions, and sought more information about who would make up the audience, they might have prepared other, more suitable jokes. For the MC and participants, therefore, knowing the possible makeup of the audience is critical. Enthusiasm in an MC is almost always welcome but you do not want to be guilty of telling the wrong joke at the wrong time to the wrong audience!

Go from Knowledge to Wisdom

Will the audience include only employees? Would there be senior executives present? Would there be many women? Would the audience be diverse in terms of age, ethnicity, or nationality? You can use this information to make your role as MC one that is broad-minded, inclusive, considerate, sensitive, and fun.

Venue

Be sure that you know the place, the venue, where you are going to serve as MC. In fact, plan to visit the location ahead of time, if possible, and while there, confirm that it is the correct place. Paying a visit to the location will help you get a better idea of how long it takes to get there. You will also be able to confirm the kind of equipment available and get a feel for the overall atmosphere. If possible, go up on stage and walk around. The more familiar you are with the stage the less nervous you will be on the day of the event.

Some cities have buildings in the same neighborhood carrying similar names. These can be fine traps for people who are new to the city or the area. For example, while you are at Dowling Centre frantically searching for the conference room where you are supposed to be the MC, two blocks down the street, on the 15th floor of Dowling Place, a roomful of people are wondering what happened to their MC!

Don't take any chances. Be sure you are at the right address and in the right building and the right room. No matter how hard you try to get to the venue, if you do not make it on time, your excuses will not be taken seriously. Being chosen as an MC entails an expectation that you will do the necessary spadework to ensure that you do not make such a simple mistake as getting lost on such an important day.

Participants/Role Takers

As an MC you will be responsible for introducing speakers, performers, and providing information, both anticipated and unanticipated. The sooner you get in touch with potential participants, the better. In addition to obtaining accurate titles of speeches or performances and clarifying how much time performers have or need, you will also need to find out how they would like to be introduced.

Performers, whether speakers, singers, or otherwise, know the value of a good introduction. Some of them might give you a package about their achievements or past record of success. It will be up to you, knowing the audience and the kind of effect you want to achieve, to select the relevant elements from each performer's background to create a welcoming introduction that makes the audience look forward to the speaker or the performer.

Some MCs like to obtain additional information from people close to the speaker or performer so that they can introduce an element of surprise. Be careful, though, because if such information is untrue, you might have the speaker correcting your comments and that is unlikely to make you feel at ease the rest of the event.

Avoid including information that is likely to embarrass the performer or the audience. Stay on higher ground.

Some MC's like to come up with a theme and use that as a basis to gather information from the speakers or performers. Perhaps, in addition to basic information about performers' achievements and other background items, an MC might ask each performer to mention his or her resolution for the coming months, assuming for example, it is toward the end of the year or the beginning of the year. Audiences will enjoy hearing the variety of responses that are interlaced with other biographical material.

Be Smooth

An MC who stumbles over words and mispronounces the name of a speaker or performer does not make a good impression. Learn how names ought to be pronounced. This may be as simple as asking the person whose name is listed on the agenda, how it is pronounced. Practice your introductions. Don't leave them to the last minute. Also, make it a point to get in touch with the person who will be introducing you as the MC to the audience and ensure that he or she has the right information about you.

Seek Pleasure from Preparation

Your attitude towards preparation can make a big difference. If you view preparation as a chore, it is unlikely that you will give your role as MC the priority and attention it deserves. Look upon preparation as an opportunity to explore and to deepen your own knowledge and extend your skills. Pour your heart into these moments of learning and discovery with the intensity and passion necessary. The payoff for intense preparation is possibly less nervousness and more confidence.

Arrive Early

An MC who arrives early on the day of the event commands respect from everybody. It becomes clear that you care about your role and respect all the participants. An MC who arrives when the event is halfway through is unlikely to be called back. Such an MC loses credibility and no excuse can make up for such lost credibility. Leave home early and allow plenty of time for delayed trains, car accidents, hurricanes, earthquakes, tornadoes, snake bites, bee swarms, and floods!

Being on time also means you can find out what changes need to be made to the agenda. It is possible that someone with a role on the agenda is unable to attend. As the MC you need to know this and find out what other alternatives might exist. Such an unanticipated change might require time to fix as it might involve asking someone else, on short notice, to fill a role. The sooner you arrive at the venue the better the chance that you can work with other stakeholders to come up with alternatives and ensure a seamless event that meets or exceeds the expectations of the audience.

Dress the Part

As the MC, you will be spending a lot of time in front of an audience. As such, members of the audience will have ample time to confirm that the stain on your tie or blouse is from the lasagna lunch you had the other day. Likewise, with your shoes on open display, wouldn't it make a better impression if they were polished? Understanding your audience and the nature of the event includes having knowledge of what it means to dress appropriately. In recent years, some corporations welcome the casual approach, meaning that if you are the MC in such a setting you might be out of place wearing a three-piece suit. On the other hand, if you are going to be the MC in a more conservative setting, appearing in your torn jeans is unlikely to make you an endearing personality. If unsure, ask those who must know, such as the one who extended the invitation to you, the level of formality expected.

Oops! I left the agenda at home!

Since you are going to leave home early, it might be a good idea to prepare what you need to take to the event the night before. Make sure that everything you need is packed and ready to go. You do not want to be searching for things in the morning or whenever you are scheduled to leave home. You are likely to forget something in such a case. Imagine arriving at the event only to realize that the program sheets you printed have been left sitting on your kitchen counter, and you are only four hours away from home while the event is starting in five minutes!

Checklist

Airline pilots use several different checklists even though they may have a lot of experience. This simply acknowledges that we are all human and that we are subject to error. By using a checklist, we make room for our fallibility. If you have a checklist such as the sample below, you can make sure that everything you need is in your bag, ready to go.

Checklist: EAST-WEST TRAIN THE TRAINER WORKSHOP
DATE: December 7, 2012

Item	Secured?
30 copies of agenda	√
Eyeglasses	√
Watch	√
Timer	X
Camera	X
Pencils	√

Make sure everything you need is in the bag. And make sure you take the right bag or briefcase!

Before the Program Starts

So, you did arrive early. Great. You have met key role takers and checked out their names on your copy of the agenda. You have made sure that agendas are strategically placed so that incoming attendees can obtain a copy. If there are name tags or name plates you have made sure that those responsible are dispensing these smoothly. You have learned about any possible changes to the program.

If the program is to start at 8:00 a.m., don't wait till 8 a.m. before you make your first appearance on the stage and connect with the audience. About five minutes to the time, approach the microphone, and remind the audience members that the program will be starting in five minutes and that they should get ready to take their seats. This announcement need not be long but you should make sure that you have been heard and that people are beginning to settle down. Remind them that the program will be starting on time. A program that starts when it is supposed to start is viewed with more respect.

Fun Spot 45: A Word to the Wise

More than anything else, I believe it's our decisions, not the conditions of our lives that determine our destiny.

~ Anthony Robbins

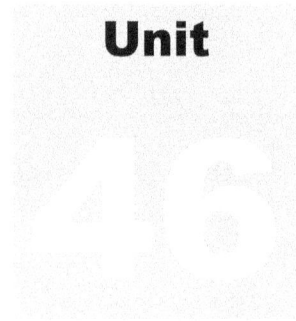

Unit 46

The MC Role: During the Event

Ladies and Gentlemen…..Welcome….

It's 7:59 a.m. and there you are at the microphone, with a big smile, poised to speak. All eyes are on you. This is not the time to fidget with your necktie or your blouse collar. Relax. All the preparation you have done is paying off in your heightened sense of confidence. Remind yourself in this brief period of anticipation to –

- **Be Bold.**

  After all, there's no turning back!

- **Be Bright.**

  You need to transform the atmosphere of the room or at least maintain the feeling of liveliness crackling in the room. Your appearance counts in this regard – both what you wear on your body and your face – your smile.

- **Be Enthusiastic.**

  You may be able to wake up those who are unsure why they are at the event and would rather be somewhere else if you show enthusiasm. Enthusiasm, after all, is infectious.

- **Be Warm.**

  You are part of the hosting team and you are going to be the person who needs to fan the embers of interest whenever it seems that attention is flagging or boredom is taking root. Don't lose your warmth halfway through the event.

With a commanding but respectful and inviting voice, begin…Ladies and gentlemen… Welcome…

Acknowledge Audience and Special Guests

All members of the audience are important and should be made to feel welcome. After all, they could have chosen to be somewhere else. Rather, they considered this event important enough for their time and they deserve respect for making this choice. Still, if there are some truly special guests, such as people in positions of power, people who have come a long way, it is a good idea to acknowledge them. This helps the audience members to know that they are in "good company" and reminds them of the importance of the event. The "celebrities" who are singled out for special mention will also feel good and are likely to have many good things to say about the event. It's a win-win-win situation.

Announce Changes in Agenda

Most events, probably, go on without changes in the agenda. If there are changes, however, such as another individual having to take on a new role or a need to change how much time is devoted to a particular item, it is best to announce it early.

Introducing the Speaker/Performer

An MC should both be able to command the attention of the audience and redirect this attention to other people such as dancers, speakers, or singers mentioned on the agenda. An MC who talks endlessly and seems to hog the limelight is very soon dismissed in the minds of the audience. The MC is necessary to get the show going but the MC is not the only important person. The more the MC is able to make others look good, the more respect the MC is likely to get.

As a reminder, the MC's introduction should be enthusiastic, tasteful, and of sufficient length. It should not be a long speech that forces the speaker or performer next on the agenda to stand forever at the sidelines with a plastic smile pasted on his or her face. Make the speaker and the audience happy to be with each other at this particular moment in time and you will have done your job well.

Smooth Segue: Look Back – Look Forward

After a presentation, the MC should acknowledge the individual and share in the applause with the audience. Saying a few fine words about the just-finished performer and the performance is in order. It makes the individual feel good going from stage to the sidelines and shows the kind of appreciation that is universally considered a hallmark of good breeding or training. That is the <u>looking back</u> part. We also need to <u>look forward.</u> And that involves providing a transition to the next speaker or performer by way of another introduction. If the MC does this well, the transition between one performance and the other will be smooth.

Be Alert

Needless to say, an MC must be highly attentive. Paying attention to a speech or performance will help the MC capture some ideas for the banter and comments before and after each performance. Such impromptu comments help to establish the MC as an attentive person. Such spontaneous humor also helps to relax audience members.

An MC has the job of getting audience members ready for one item after another. An MC, therefore, needs to be "present" in the sense of knowing exactly which part of the program is currently unfolding. An MC who forgets names or titles of speeches does not seem to be on top of her game.

On Your Toes – Keeping Time

One of the MC's most important tasks is ensuring that the program adheres to time. In some cases, there may be another group using your venue shortly after your agreed-upon closing time. If you do not finish on time, you will have other people standing outside (if you are lucky) waiting for you or (if you are unlucky) you will have a group of people banging on the door of the room, disrupting the last few most important moments of your event. It will be no fun at all if you have to rush through the last few items on your schedule. You will also not be happy having dozens of people breathing down your neck as you try to wrap up. In short, if your event runs overtime, it is going to be an inconvenience to others, make a bad impression about event organizers, and adversely affect participants or audience members who have other equally important commitments elsewhere.

A good MC will craft the agenda with a small measure of flexibility while at the same time making sure that all role-takers adhere to their time commitments. If there are small discrepancies in time, the MC can make up for them by either filling time with adlibbed comments or shorten introductory comments where too much time has been taken elsewhere. Ideally, others will stick closely to the agenda but in truth, this is not always the case. If participants are briefed beforehand regarding the importance of time, one might hope that they will strictly adhere to the time requirements. Usually, when participants are aware that there are provisions for cutting short a performance or speech, they will endeavor to work within the time. Use a timing device, such as a color-coded card that you raise up at predetermined times or a bell (not too loud!), to alert speakers and performers. Of course, the MC herself does not have to do this. You can appoint someone to handle this highly important task. In any case, it is the responsibility of the MC to make sure that the program proceeds according to the agenda. An MC is a leader. Leadership comes with responsibility and requires making executive decisions. Such decisions may be difficult at times such as having to cut short a speech but they are decisions that might have to be made at times, for the greater good. Good luck. An MC who feels forced to cut short a speech or performance will do well to offer some soothing comments to help the individual involved overcome any bad feelings engendered by the move.

The MC's Prepared Comments

Using the agenda, the MC can prepare some comments for strategic moments throughout the event. The MC should be flexible enough to add to or delete from these comments when necessary. At the initial stages of preparation an MC might want to write down exact comments for each portion of the event. This is a good way to ensure that your comments are concise and concentrated to achieve maximum effect. If you try to wing it, there is a chance you may be longwinded, taking too much time and contributing to an overrun. Comedians, magicians, actors, all plan their words and actions carefully. Why not you as an MC?

MC's Notes

An MC caught behind a lectern reading notes to the audience is not a pretty sight. If the MC only has brief points (key words and phrases) to refer to, this can allow for much more of a sense of spontaneity and sound less scripted. With that in mind, check out the next unit, which uses the East-West Train the Trainer agenda introduced in Unit 45, to introduce how you might whittle down your comments as an MC from full sentences to point form.

Fun Spot 46: A Word to the Wise

Great minds have purposes: others have wishes.

~ Washington Irving

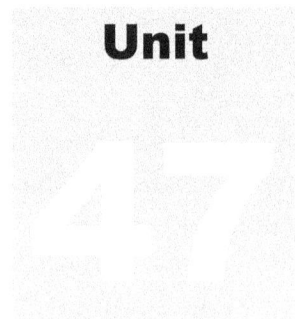

The MC Role: Bringing the Agenda to Life

Here below is a sample agenda. An agenda need not be fancy. It needs to be clear and well laid out.

<u>AGENDA</u>

8:00 a.m.	Welcome/Coffee & Tea	
8:30	Session opens	Mr. Ping-Ping Tang (MC)
8:35	Company president's remarks	Ms. Erika Yamataka
8:45 (2 hours)	Negotiation Mastery Workshop	Ms. Fatima Springsteen
10:45	Break (15 minutes)	
11:00 (2 hours)	Karma & Charisma	Mr. Vikas Van der Hoof
1:00 p.m.	Close	
1:05	Photo session	
1:15	Free lunch	

Agenda with MC Notes (written out in full)

	MC's Comments <u>Before</u> Agenda Item	Agenda Item	Participants	MC's Comments <u>After</u> Agenda Item
8:00 am		Welcome/ Coffee & Tea		
8:25	Ladies and Gentlemen. Thanks for coming. The program is about to start. Please take your seats. Please take your seats. Thank you.			
8:30	Good morning. Welcome one and all to this highly-anticipated training session. We have a marvelous program for you and it is great to see that you were all able to make it. Before the official welcome from the president, Ms. Erika Yamataka, I want to draw your attention to one item on the agenda. At 11 am, the workshop on Karma and Charisma will be handled not only by Mr. Vikas Van der Hoof but also one of his partners, Swami Yamanakananda. We are very fortunate to have these highly charismatic professionals in our midst today.	Session Opens	Mr. Ping-Ping Tang (MC)	
8:35	Now, President Erika Yamataka has always been very conscious of the value of training, which is why we have this incredible opportunity today. It is my pleasure to present to you, the president of East-West, Ms. Erika Yamataka!	Company president's remarks	Ms. Erika Yamataka	Thank you very much. Ms. Yamataka for those words of wisdom and encouragement. I am sure that all the workshop participants are eagerly looking forward to how they can sharpen their negotiation skills. Thank you.
8:45	Negotiation is a fact of daily life, whether we are in the boardroom, on the playground, or at home with our family. Today, we are very fortunate to have with us someone who has devoted a lifetime to studying and practicing negotiation at the very highest levels. Ms. Fatima Springsteen has been personally involved in labor dispute negotiations, national reconciliation negotiations, and even negotiations for the release of hostages. Hopefully, you will never need to use your negotiation skills for that kind of delicate situation but there is much that we can learn from her to make us successful in our business interactions and negotiations. Ladies and gentlemen, won't you help me give a big, big hand of welcome to Ms. Fatima Springsteen!	Negotiation Mastery Workshop	Ms. Fatima Springsteen	Wow! Thanks very much Ms. Springsteen for a spirited workshop. I never thought negotiation could be so much fun and I am sure I echo the sentiments of all participants if I say that this has been one of the most enjoyable experiences in our work life. Ladies and gentlemen, how about another big round of applause for a master negotiator and teacher! (Lead the applause)

Guaranteed Formula for Public Speaking

	MC's Comments <u>Before</u> Agenda Item	Agenda Item	Participants	MC's Comments <u>After</u> Agenda Item
10:45	You must all be looking forward to a little bit of downtime for refreshment. Let's take a 15 minute break. My time now is 10:47 a.m. We are running a little bit behind so would you kindly return to this room at 11 a.m. We are shaving 2 minutes off our break so that we can finish on time. Thank you for your cooperation and please be in your seats by 11 am. OK, break time!	Break		
10:59	Please take your seats. Thank you. Please take your seats so that we can start on time. Thank you very much.			
11:00	Welcome back. The break may have been short but keep in mind that we are going to have a free lunch. I hear it's going to be really good. Two years ago, I had the benefit of taking a workshop led by Mr. Vikas Van der Hoof on the subject of Dressing from the Inside Out. It's one of the best experiences of my life and so I feel that it is such a wondrous opportunity for all of us to have this chance to learn from both Mr. Vikas Van der Hoof and his business associate Swami Yamanakananda on how we can apply concepts of karma and charisma to revive not only our personal fortunes but also make a difference in our company's contributions to the world. Ladies and gentlemen, please join me in giving a wholehearted welcome to two of the best business coaches of our generation, Mr. Vikas Van der Hoof and Swami Yamakananda! (Lead the applause)	Karma & Charisma	Mr. Vikas Van der Hoof & Swami Yamanak-ananda	Thank you. Thank you. Thank you so much, Mr. Van der Hoof and Swami Yamanakananda, for helping us gain new insights into how we attract and repel those around us. It is revealing how much power we have that we are not aware of. We also thank you for your patience in explaining some of the more challenging terms and we look forward very much to applying these principles in the days and months to come. Thank you. (Lead the applause)
1:00 pm	I would like to thank all the participants, President Yamataka, and all our session leaders, Ms. Fatima Springsteen, Mr. Vikas Van der Hoof and Swami Yamanakananda for their efforts in opening our eyes to new possibilities in both the personal and professional realms. I hope that you will take these skills and make the most of them. We have a photo session in this room and just outside. This will take about ten minutes, after which you can all make your way to the lunch area. Thank you all for coming! (Lead the applause)	Close	MC	
1:05		Photo session		
1:15		Free lunch		

Agenda with MC Notes (point form)

	MC's Comments Before Agenda Item	Agenda Item	Participants	MC's Comments After Agenda Item
8:00 am		Welcome/ Coffee/Tea		
8:25	Start / Welcome / Take seats.			
8:30	Highly-anticipated / welcome to all change in agenda item 11 am workshop (Mr. Vikas Van der Hoof + Swami Yamanakananda	Session Opens	Mr. Ping-Ping Tang (MC)	
8:35	President Erika Yamataka/value of training Pleasure to present Pres. (lead applause)	Company president's remarks	Ms. Erika Yamataka	Thanks 4 insights / all eager / sharpen persona/prof. image
8:45	Negotiation/ fact of daily life fortunate / someone / lifetime studying and practicing negotiation Ms. Fatima Springsteen / labor dispute negotiations, national reconciliation negotiations, hostage release learn from her / successful in business interactions and negotiations. big hand of welcome to Ms. Fatima Springsteen!	Negotiation Mastery Workshop	Ms. Fatima Springsteen	- Thanks Ms. Springsteen (Lead the applause)
10:45	- Looking forward to refreshment - 15 minute break/in yr seats by 11 am	Break		
10:59	Call participants to seats.			
11:00	Welcome back Reminder / free lunch / 1:30 pm 2 yrs ago/ workshop/ Mr. Van der Hoof (Dressing from the Inside Out). Learning chance - 4 personal & professional growth Should make difference in our company Mr. Vikas Van der Hoof and Swami Yamakananda!	Karma & Charisma	Mr. Vikas Van der Hoof & Swami Yamanakananda	Thank you new insights re: attract/repel personal power revealed - Knowledge - Thank you. (Lead the applause)
1:00	Thanks, Pres. Yamataka Ms. Fatima Springsteen, Mr. Vikas Van der Hoof and Swami Yamanakananda new possibilities photo session (10 minutes) free lunch (1:15 pm) Thank you all!	Close	MC	
1:05 pm		Photo session		
1:15		Free lunch		

Fun Spot 47: A Word to the Wise

Success is determined not by whether or not you face obstacles, but by your reaction to them. And if you look at these obstacles as a containing fence, they become your excuse for failure. If you look at them as a hurdle, each one strengthens you for the next.

~ Ben Carson (Gifted Hands: The Ben Carson Story)

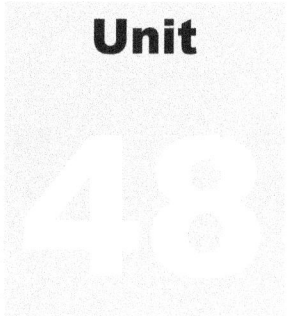

Unit 48

The MC Role: After the Event

Be sociable. Make an effort to talk to participants and role-takers. This can be a networking opportunity for all concerned. You may be able to extend a helping hand to someone you meet at the event just as someone might become an important contact for you in the future.

Express your appreciation to the sponsors and those who invited you. You may do so by writing a letter, sending an email or making a telephone call. Also, seek feedback so that you can improve your performance.

Fun Spot 48: A Word to the Wise

The most important persuasion tool you have

in your entire arsenal is integrity.

~ Zig Ziglar

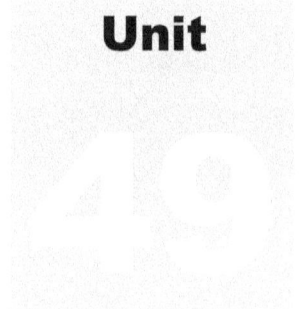

Unit 49

Public Speaking – Going Pro

> The ability to speak is a shortcut to distinction. It puts a person in the limelight, raises one head and shoulders above the crowd.
>
> - Lowell Thomas
> (Introduction to Dale Carnegie's book, *How to Win Friends and Influence People*)

You may not harbor the goal of becoming a professional speaker who travels around the world dispensing wisdom and insight. Within your personal and professional sphere, however, there may be numerous opportunities to deliver speeches or to share your ideas with others. Even though you may not consider yourself a professional in the sense of making your full-time living from public speaking, this does not mean that you should not aspire to professional level performance. You certainly want your work presentations to be of professional level quality, don't you?

Anyone who takes the time to come and listen to a speech or to participate in a meeting or forum expects good use of that time. Thus, if you are the one on the podium giving the speech, you would want to give the very best of yourself. Likewise, if you find yourself in the role of an MC you would do well to ensure that the event progresses in a smooth manner while projecting all the role-takers in the best possible light so that they can feel comfortable enough to give of their best to the audience.

If you decide to ease into professional speaking, there are a number of tried and true ways by which you can make the transition. This does not necessarily mean quitting your day job, however. You can enjoy life as a public speaker without giving up your main occupation. In fact, oftentimes, the experience you have acquired from your profession could very well be the springboard for launching you into the world of professional speaking. At the very least, you can commit yourself to sharing knowledge with others. The payback is that the more public speaking you do, the better you will get.

Join a Speakers Association

Your professional group (accounting, engineering, medicine, law?) may offer opportunities for speakers to impart their knowledge to various groups or schools. For example, members of writers groups such as the Society of Children's Book Writers can make themselves available to speak at schools or school-related events or to aspiring authors. Such opportunities can snowball if you prove yourself engaging, informative, or entertaining.

Request Free Speaking Opportunities

If you are at the beginning of your speaking career, nobody knows about you. So, you have to make people aware of you. You can do this by writing a letter introducing yourself to a target group and including some of the topics you are interested in talking about. If your package is professionally designed, it is possible that you will attract some groups curious enough to give you a chance. If such groups understand that they do not have to pay you, they might be willing to give you the chance. As you establish a good reputation, you will find that more and more groups will request your speaking services and even offer to pay you.

Record Your Presentations

If possible, get out the video camera and record your presentations. You can learn from these recordings yourself and you can share them with those who want to learn from you or benefit from what you have to offer. Your past successes can encourage others to give you a chance. Putting some of your efforts on the Internet such as on YouTube can make it easy for others to observe how dynamic you are as a speaker. More than that, you can use such recordings as a learning tool and profit by learning from your errors.

Request Feedback

When you request feedback from an organization that has made use of your speaking or MC skills, you may get a thank-you letter, which can add to your list of testimonials. At the same time, any feedback you get can allow you to build on your skills and to reach out for another level of excellence as a speaker.

Fun Spot 49: A Word to the Wise

Other people's opinion of you

does not have to

become your reality.

~ Les Brown

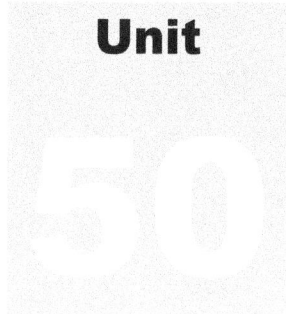

Resources

Continued Public Speaking Skills Development

1) Dale Carnegie Training (founded 1912)

   Over 75 countries
   Focus on:
   - Leadership
   - Public speaking
   - Selling

   www.dalecarnegie.com

2) PowerTalk International (founded 1938 as International Toastmistress Clubs)

   Focus on:
   - Presentations
   - Parliamentary Procedures
   - Conference and Function Planning
   - Public speaking

   www.powertalkinternational.com

3) Toastmasters International (Founded 1924)

   Non profit group
   Focus on:
   - Leadership
   - Public speaking
   - Selling

   www.toastmasters.org

Fun Spot 50: A Word to the Wise

Doing what you love is the cornerstone of having abundance in your life.

~ Dr. Wayne Dyer

Bibliography

Bass, Carole. "As Nanotech's Promise Grows, Will Puny Particles Present Big Problems?" *Scientific American*, February 15, 2008.

Carnegie, Dale. *How to Win Friends and Influence People*. NY, NY: Simon and Schuster, 2009.

Carnegie, Dale. *Public Speaking and Influencing Men in Business*. Kessinger Publishing, 2003.

Gore, Al. "Global Warming is an Immediate Crisis." Wednesday, 20 September 2006. Speech to New York University School of Law. http://www.algore.org

Prusher, Ilene. Well-ordered homelessness: life on Japan's fringe. *The Christian Science Monitor*. May 14, 2001.

Spence, Gerry. *How to Argue and Win Every Time*. NY, NY: St. Martin's Press, 1995.

Tatami http://www.en.wikipedia.org/wiki/Tatami

Recommended Books

Name of Author	Book title	Publisher/Year
Dale Carnegie	The Quick and Easy Way to Effective Speaking	2002
Gerry Spence	How to Argue and Win Every time.	1995
Jeff Slutsky, Michael Aun	Toastmaster's International Guide to Successful Speaking: Overcoming Your Fears, Winning over Your Audience, Building Your Business & Career	1996
Joan Detz	How to Write and Give a Speech, Second Revised Edition: A Practical Guide For Executives, PR People, the Military, Fund-Raisers, Politicians, Educators, and Anyone Who Has to Make Every Word Count	2002
Lilly Walters	Secrets of Successful Speaker: How You can Motivate, Captivate, and Persuade	1993
Lilly Walters	Secrets of Superstar Speakers: Wisdom from the Greatest Motivators of our Time	2000
Lilly Walters	What to Say When: A Complete Resource for Speakers, Trainers and Executives	1995
Lenny Laskowski, Princeton Language Institute	10 Days to More Confident Public Speaking	2009
Stephen E. Lucas	The Art of Public Speaking	2009

Useful Websites

Guidelines for Public Speaking
http://faculty.baruch.cuny.edu/shannah/blsci2/publicspeaking.pdf

Introducing a Speaker
http://www.toastmasters.org.nz/index.cfm/Speaking_Resources/Introductions.html

Public Speaking Tips
http://www.actingforbusiness.com/publicspeaking/generalpublic/publicspeakingtips/PublicSpeakingTips.htm

Speech Introductions and Conclusions: Some "Do's" and "Don'ts"
James Helmer, Oral Communication Center, Hamilton College
http://academics.hamilton.edu/occ/intro_conclusion.pdf

Ten Tips for Successful Public Speaking
http://www.toastmasters.org/pdfs/105.pdf

Templates

MC – Pre-departure Checklist – Add to the list

Item	Secured?
Copy/copies of agenda	
Watch	
Timer	
Pencils/Pens	

Introducing a Speaker (preparation sheet):

Name of speaker: _____

Speech title (if any): _____

_____

Why the issue is important to the audience: _____

_____

Why the speaker is qualified to speak on this topic: _____

_____

_____

Introduction text (beginning, middle, end):

_____

_____

_____

_____

_____

_____

_____

(LEAD THE APPLAUSE/START CLAPPING!!!)

Speech Evaluation Form (CR Technique)

Intro:

Commendation (C): Issue + Why

C: Issue + Why

Recommendation (R): Issue + Why

Summary:

Sandwich Evaluation Technique Template

Positive point:

Point of growth:

Positive point:

Positive point:

Point of growth:

Positive point:

Short Notice Speech Preparation Template

Title: _____

Introduction (including 3 points you want to highlight)	
Point 1	
Point 2	
Point 3	
Conclusion	

Evaluating with IMGEPaC - Template

Evaluator's Opening Statement	
I – INTRODUCTION	
M – MESSAGE	
G – GESTURES	
E – EYE CONTACT	
Pa – PAUSING/PACING	
C – CONCLUSION	
Evaluator's Concluding Statement	

100 Topics for Impromptu Speaking Practice

1	Exercise	26	Patience
2	Happiness	27	School uniforms
3	Travel	28	Magic
4	Food	29	Dinosaurs
5	Peace	30	Being between jobs
6	Leadership	31	Unity
7	Miscommunication	32	Imagination
8	Fantasy	33	Jury
9	Einstein	34	Astrology
10	Mystery	35	Diversity
11	Luck	36	Coffee
12	Favorite writer	37	Friends in common
13	Good memories	38	Negotiation
14	Justice	39	Extreme sports
15	Circus	40	Aliens
16	Conflict	41	Oil
17	Advertisements	42	Debating
18	Marathon	43	Seeing is believing
19	Entrepreneurship	44	Intuition
20	Persistence	45	Sharks
21	Traditions	46	Solar energy
22	Manners	47	Yoga
23	Amazon jungle	48	iPad
24	Distance learning	49	Chess
25	Hobbies	50	Friends

51	Meditation	76	Beauty contests
52	The elderly	77	Nature
53	Multilingualism	78	Retirement
54	Fun stuff	79	Global village
55	Taxi drivers	80	Zoos
56	Snow	81	Disney
57	Dreams	82	Favorite movie
58	Golf	83	Surfing
59	Twitter	84	Whale watching
60	News online	85	Politicians who shed tears in public
61	Horse racing	86	Fads
62	Democracy	87	Competition
63	Honey	88	Teamwork
64	Credit cards	89	Comedy
65	Safety	90	Knowledge
66	Finders keepers	91	Astronomy
67	Power	92	Favorite color
68	The beach	93	Dictatorship
69	What I believe…	94	Experience is the best teacher
70	Vegetarianism	95	Art
71	Diamonds	96	Electric cars
72	Computer literacy	97	Farming
73	Serendipity	98	European Union
74	Contracts	99	Speed
75	Wine	100	The Eiffel Tower

Index

A
Acronyms, 5, 150
Agenda, 53, 157, 158, 160, 161, 162, 165, 166, 167, 168, 169, 171, 182
Alliteration, 75
Anecdotes, 11, 22, 38, 44, 47, 64, 67, 68, 70, 73, 87, 103, 104

B
Bait and Switch, 143, 144
Bass, Carole, 132
Big Apple, 41
Body language, 10, 30
Brazil, 148
Brown, Les, 176
Bush, George W., 122, 123

C
Capitalists, 144, 145
Carson, Ben Dr., 172
China, People's Republic of, 8
Chinese, 99, 100
Chocolate, 140
Chronos, 9
Churchill, Winston, 2, 99, 100, 136
Clinton, Hillary, 74, 106
Commendation, 43, 91, 92, 94, 97, 104
Communists, 144, 145
Confucius, 144
Coolangatta, 15, 16
Criticism, 54, 55, 60, 123

D
Definition, 5, 32, 74, 76
Demonstrative, 27
Dialogue, 64, 75
Doraemon, 144

E
Egypt, 149
English, 1, 6
Eye contact, 31, 34, 38, 45, 58, 59, 91, 97, 116, 118, 119, 153, 187

F
Facts, 28, 67, 68, 74, 121
Feedback, 1, 4, 45, 54, 55, 62, 91, 96, 117, 173, 175
Feminists, 144, 145
Figures, 67, 74, 144

G
Gandhi, 144
Gold Coast, 15, 16, 103
Golf, 22, 23, 189
Greenpeace, 144

H
Hawaii, 44, 121
Humorous, 27, 28, 44, 159
Hyperbole, 75

I
Informative, 27, 44, 175
Irony, 64, 74
Irving, Washington, 167

J
Japan, v, 22, 47, 73, 131, 132, 144, 179
Jesus, 144

K
Kennedy, John F. 196, 125
King, Martin Luther Jr., 66

M
Maglev, 74
Manga, 144
Master of Ceremonies, 155
Memorizing, 51
Metaphor, 74, 87, 88, 100
Monet, 100
Monroe, Marilyn, 79

N
Nakura, Seiji, 100
Narrative, 127
NASA, 19, 20
Nigeria, 148
Nobel Prize, 121
Noonan, Peggy, 115

O
Obama, Barack, 74, 99, 100, 125, 126
Onomatopoeia, 75
Ownby, Matthew, 153
Oxfam, 79

P
Pacing, 30, 34, 38, 59, 116, 118, 119, 187
Paradox, 75
Parallelism, 76
Pausing, 27, 30, 59, 116, 118, 119, 187
Personification, 75
Persuasive, 27, 28, 121, 122
Picasso, 100
Powell, Colin, 123
Prime Minister, 8, 46
Putonghua, 6

R
Recommendation, 43, 91, 92, 94, 97, 184
Rhetorical question(s), 12, 13, 64, 70, 74, 79, 153
Rohn, Jim, 135
Rule of Three, 68
Russian, 8

S
Samurai, 137, 144, 146
Sarnoff, Dorothy, 130
Scandinavian, 145
Signposting, 38, 44
Similes, 64, 74, 88
Spanish, 6
Spence, Gerry, 103, 179, 180
Statistics, 11, 38, 67, 87
Sumo, 47, 74
Super Bowl, 134

T
Talese, Gay, 67
Tatami, 131, 132, 179
Thatcher, Margaret, 101
Thesis statement, 87, 88
Toastmasters Club, v, vii, 177, 181
Totoro, 144
Twain, Mark, 124

U
UK, 88
United States, 20, 106, 122, 123, 145
Uranium, 8, 9
Urdu, 6

V
Van Gogh, Vincent, 70, 100
Vocal variety, 27, 30, 106, 153

W
Weak point, 33, 56
Wrestling, 33, 47

Y
Yasuda, Hitoshi, 100

Z
Ziglar, Zig, 173

About the Author

Everett Ofori holds an MBA from Heriot-Watt University (Scotland, UK). He teaches Writing, Public Speaking and English for International Communication. Everett has helped hundreds of high school and university students around the world to improve their writing and grades. He has worked extensively with business executives but is equally at home with helping young people hone their writing skills.

Note to Users:

If you have any comments regarding this book or wish to present any ideas for improving the work, please contact the author, Everett Ofori, at one of the following:

Email: everettofori@gmail.com

Mailing address:

Everett Ofori

Takarazuka University of Art and Design

Tokyo Campus Bldg 1F, 123 (MBE)

7-11-1 Nishi Shinjuku

Shinjuku ku, Tokyo Japan

160-0023

Notes

Notes

Notes

Notes

www.ingramcontent.com/pod-product-compliance
Lightning Source LLC
Chambersburg PA
CBHW081348160426
43202CB00016B/2916